Praise for *Total Heart Health for Men*

"Spiritual and physical fitness honors God and energizes us for the challenges of life. The 'heart team' of Drs. Young, Duncan, and Leachman, inspire and motivate men (and the women who love them) to get and stay healthy and live an abundant life each day. All of us should say yes to the challenge of strengthening our hearts, lengthening our lives and glorifying God with total health."

> — JACK GRAHAM
> Pastor, Prestonwood Baptist
> Church, Plano, TX

"*Total Heart Health for Men* is a clear, convicting, and comprehensive study of the heart of a man. Addressing both the spiritual and physical health of the male heart, the authors deliver a total package for achieving excellence as a man for the glory of God and the good of those we love."

> — DANIEL L. AKIN
> President, Southeastern Baptist
> Theological Seminary

"Since you only get one heart, it's a good idea to take care of it! I can't think of better guys to write about the importance of keeping ourselves fit from the inside out. Especially since one of them is my friend, Ed Young, who has helped me—and hundreds of thousands of others—keep their hearts strong for Jesus Christ."

> — DR. JOSEPH M. STOWELL
> Teaching Pastor,
> Harvest Bible Chapel

"God created us as body/soul unities. Thus we are not mere material men. As good stewards, we must care for both the physical and non-physical aspects of our humanity. As such, *Total Heart Health for Men* is just what the doctor ordered. Drs. Young, Duncan, and Leachman explain exactly what we men must do to develop bodies and souls fit for the Master's service!"

> — HANK HANEGRAAFF
> President, Christian Research
> Institute and host of the *Bible
> Answer Man* broadcast

"Drs. Young, Duncan, and Leachman have produced a book that every man needs to read. Using their extensive knowledge and experience, they have provided a resource that every man can use to have a better quality of life, both spiritually and physically. No matter where you are in the stages of life, you will find this book to be a great help. I highly recommend it and plan to provide copies for every man on our staff."

— MIKE HAMLET
Pastor, First Baptist Church,
North Spartanburg, SC

"Anyone who has known me for any length of time knows how seriously I take heart health. And I give much of the credit for my heart-healthy attitude to one of the authors of this book—a man who also happens to be my father. Through this great book, Dad and his two co-authors, Drs. Duncan and Leachman, provide men an invaluable tool to ramp up both their physical and spiritual health. Men, I urge you to 'take to heart' the thoroughly-researched and timely advice in this book . . . it may just save your life!"

— ED YOUNG
Senior Pastor,
Fellowship Church and author,
The Creative Leader

"An informative book rich in medical detail by an esteemed group of authors. It's a book that will capture your attention if you're like most overweight adults. Personally, I've strived to honor Christ spiritually, but I've failed to honor Him physically. This book has encouraged me to significantly improve my physical well-being. Hopefully I can remain motivated!"

— ARCHIE DUNHAM
Retired Chairman/CEO of
Conoco/Phillips

Total Heart Health
for Men

Dr. Ed Young

Dr. Michael Duncan and Dr. Richard Leachman

W PUBLISHING GROUP
A Division of Thomas Nelson Publishers
Since 1798

www.wpublishinggroup.com

Published by W Publishing Group, a Division of Thomas Nelson, Inc., P.O. Box 141000, Nashville, Tennessee 37214. Authors are represented by the literary agency of WordServe Literary Group, 2235 Ashwood Place, Highlands Ranch, Colorado 80129.

W Publishing Group books may be purchased in bulk for educational, business, fund-raising, or sales promotional use. For information, please e-mail SpecialMarkets@ThomasNelson.com.

Unless otherwise noted, when first names only appear, they are fictitious names for real people or for composites of real people. Identifying details have been changed to protect anonymity. Any resemblance is purely coincidental.

All Scripture quotations, unless otherwise indicated, are taken from the New American Standard Bible®. Copyright © 1960, 1962, 1963, 1968, 1971, 1972, 1973, 1975, 1977, 1995 by The Lockman Foundation. Used by permission.

Other Scripture references are from the following sources:

The Message (MSG) by Eugene H. Peterson. Copyright © 1993, 1994, 1995, 1996, 2000, 2001, 2002. Used by permission of NavPress Publishing Group. All rights reserved.

The *Holy Bible*, New Living Translation® (NLT®). Copyright © 1996. Used by permission of Tyndale House Publishers, Inc., Wheaton, Illinois 60189. All rights reserved.

The King James Version (KJV). Public domain.

Library of Congress Cataloging-in-Publication Data

Young, Ed
    Total heart health for men / Ed Young, Michael Duncan, and Richard Leachman.
      p. cm.
    Includes bibliographical references.
    ISBN 0-8499-0013-1
    1. Heart—Diseases—Popular works. 2. Men—Health and hygiene—Popular works.
I. Leachman, Richard. II. Duncan, Michael, M.D. III. Title.
RC672.Y682 2005
616.1'205'081—dc22   2005022147

Printed in the United States of America

05 06 07 08 QW 9 8 7 6 5 4 3 2 1

IMPORTANT CAUTION—PLEASE READ THIS!

The principles and practices recommended in this book result from the research and experiences of the authors. However, the reader is strongly cautioned to consult with his or her personal physician *before* initiating any changes in physical lifestyle. While the Total Heart Health approach has proved effective for many people in improving overall heart health, it is not intended as a strategy for curing serious heart disease. The reader should not use this book as the ultimate source of information about the subject of the book.

This book is sold without warranties of any kind, express or implied, and the publisher and authors disclaim any liability, loss, or damage caused by the contents of this book.

CONTENTS

Contents

Part 3: The Foundation Stones for Strengthening a Man's Heart

Man to Man, Heart to Heart

Don't leave the health of your total heart to chance.

Dr. Ed Young

During a Hawaiian vacation not too long ago, I was playing golf with two doctors on one of the world's most magnificent courses. Dr. Mike Duncan, Dr. Rick Leachman, and their wives are members of the church where I am senior pastor. The two couples had joined my wife, Jo Beth, and me on the island of Maui for a few days of fun in the sun, and playing golf in Hawaii is about as good as it gets.

The golf course stretches along the shoulders of a ridge hoisted up from the sea eons ago by volcanic fury. Brilliant green fairways bordered by towering Norfolk pines and swaying palms flow into the bright blue of the sky above and the deep cobalt of the ocean below. It always seems like my drives fly straighter and farther when I play in Hawaii. And even when they don't, who really cares when you're playing in a place like this?

As we golfed, our conversation eventually drifted to our respective professions and the needs of the people we help day by day. I listened with deep interest as Mike, a cardiovascular surgeon, and Rick, an interventional cardiologist, talked about heart disease, America's number one killer. They admitted that many of the patients who come to them need angioplasty, bypass surgery, or a heart transplant because they have ignored good habits of diet and exercise.

I knew exactly what they were talking about. About seventeen years ago, I was rushed to the emergency room after experiencing chest pains and numbness in my arms while riding a stationary bike. Doctors discovered that my left anterior descending artery was blocked. Thankfully, I didn't need open-heart surgery. Angioplasty successfully reopened the blocked artery. So when Mike and Rick talked about people needing to take good care of their "tickers," in my case they were preaching to the choir!

When I talked about my work, the topic was still the heart. Even though I've learned a lot about the physical heart since my near miss with a heart attack, my primary frame of reference is the spiritual heart. I have devoted my life to helping people connect with God and grow in spiritual health. And just as the patients of my doctor friends often come to them only when problems arise, many of the people who come to me for help struggle with spiritual problems, having either overlooked or ignored principles and habits of spiritual heart health.

As Mike, Rick, and I talked and chased golf balls, it suddenly hit us: all three of us were "heart doctors." We had dedicated our lives to helping men and women enjoy happy, productive lives by maintaining healthy hearts. We agreed that the fitness of both the physical heart *and* the spiritual heart is vital to overall health. It's not enough to have a healthy body if the soul is sick or anemic. Nor is it sufficient to be spiritually strong while neglecting the physical heart. But if care is taken to maintain a lifestyle of spiritual and physical heart health, quality and enjoyment of life—Total Heart Health—is the result.

I don't remember which hole we were playing when we started joking about the three of us "experts" collaborating on a book on the topic of a Total Heart Health lifestyle. But before the round was finished, we were talking seriously about it. We decided to merge our expertise in the two vital areas of physical heart health and spiritual heart health to encourage people toward *Total Heart Health*. I don't recall what I shot that day, and it really doesn't matter. That Maui vacation resulted in the principles we have developed and shared with others through the Total Heart Health resources.

A Life-Changing Episode

My heart episode was a major wake-up call for Jo Beth and me. Our lives changed drastically. We began not only practicing the principles for heart health you will read about in this book, but also encouraging others to do so as well. We are so committed to Total Heart Health at our church, that we have a worship center, a fully equipped fitness center, and a café serving healthy meals—all under the same roof! We are equally committed to healthy physical hearts and healthy spiritual hearts.

I can say with confidence that if you implement the principles presented in these pages, *your life will be changed as well!* Jo Beth and I are living proof, as are hundreds of men and women in our community who have adopted the Total Heart Health lifestyle. We will show you how to replace bad health habits with a good health lifestyle in 90 days. This Total Heart Health lifestyle will transform you inside and out, heart and soul. It's our 90-Day Challenge to you.

I may be better educated about the physical heart than most men, thanks to a life-changing trip to the ER. But I'm no expert. My writing partners, however, *are* experts on the human heart. They are two of the most respected heart specialists in the country.

Dr. Michael Duncan is associate surgeon at the Texas Heart Institute (THI). He is also clinical associate professor, Department of Surgery, at the University Medical School at Houston, and director of the Cardiovascular Fellowship Program at THI. Dr. Duncan studied under two of the world's most famous heart specialists, Dr. Michael DeBakey and Dr. Denton Cooley. Mike has extensive experience in performing all types of cardiovascular procedures, including coronary artery bypass and heart valve surgery. He has performed more than one hundred heart transplants. Mike and his wife, Patsy, have two sons and devote many hours to our church's medical team.

Dr. Rick Leachman is equally qualified in his knowledge of the heart. He's an interventional cardiologist and partner with Leachman Cardiology Associates, an affiliate of THI and St. Luke's Episcopal Hospital, Houston. Rick also is associate chief of cardiology at St. Luke's and medical director of THI's Cardiac Catherization Laboratory. In addition, Rick works as clinical associate professor of medicine, Baylor College of Medicine and The University of Texas Health Science Center at Houston. Rick is fluent in Spanish and Italian as well as his native English, which is helpful as he serves a wide variety of patients in the huge Texas Medical Center in Houston. He and his wife, Marcy, have two daughters and a son.

Two special women play important roles in this book. Jo Beth, my wife, shares our desire to help people embrace a Total Heart Health lifestyle. Part of her interest comes from having to endure my cardiac episode in 1988. For more than forty years, Jo Beth has been my partner in helping people develop strong spiritual hearts. Later in this book, she will join me for a special word to women aimed at helping them encourage the men in their lives in the pursuit of Total Heart Health.

In this book, you will also meet Kristy Brown, who works with both men and women as the physical fitness director at the Family Life Center of Second Baptist Church, Houston. Kristy graduated from college with a major in health and physical fitness. She is also certified by the American College of Sports Medicine, the Cooper Institute for Aerobic Research, and the Aerobics and Fitness Association of America, among others. Kristy wrote chapter 15 of this book, which focuses on exercise.

Most important, we are all students of the Bible. We believe that to enjoy Total Heart Health you must take care of the heart in its totality—spiritual and physical.

A Strategy for Your Total Heart Health

In order to encourage you to adopt a Total Heart Health lifestyle, my partners and I set before you what we call the 90-Day Challenge. We compare the three stages of this challenge to the three stages for getting a NASA shuttle off the launch pad and into earth orbit. The whole process takes only a matter of minutes, as booming rockets catapult a space crew into the heavens. Launching a new lifestyle doesn't happen as quickly. We believe that getting into a Total Heart Health lifestyle takes about 90 days, with stage transitions at around 21 and 45 days.

Lifting Off

The first stage of the shuttle launch is getting the space vehicle off the ground. This is accomplished primarily by two massive solid rocket boosters (SRB), which displace about 6.6 million pounds of thrust and provide more than 70 percent of the power at liftoff. SRB separation occurs at about 150,000 feet or twenty-four nautical miles downrange, having delivered the orbiter from much of earth's gravitational pull on its way into orbit. In a similar way, *the first three weeks of the Total Heart Health plan will help you soar free of destructive old habits and replace them with healthy new habits.*

For example, implementing our dietary recommendations will help you establish new patterns for eating the right foods in the right quantities. You will also be prompted to get into a program of daily exercise that's right for you. And you will be encouraged and coached to carve out daily time to connect with God.

Many behavioral experts claim that it takes twenty-one days of repetition to break a habit and establish another one. After about three weeks of practicing healthy physical and spiritual disciplines, you should sense that you have established a positive, healthy new "groove" for your life.

We trust that reading this book will provide "ignition" for your launch off the pad. These pages are filled with proven principles and helpful examples for both physical and spiritual heart health. Block out some serious reading time during the next week or so to work through what Mike, Rick, Jo Beth, Kristy, and I have to share.

In this book, we address the health needs of the physical heart and spiritual heart simultaneously. You will notice at the beginning of each chapter one or two symbols, indicating the emphasis of that chapter. Chapters marked with the symbol on the left focus more on the spiritual heart. Chapters marked with the sybol on the right emphasize physical heart health. And chapters marked with both symbols, such as this one, are intersections of the physical and spiritual heart.

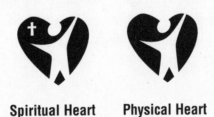

Spiritual Heart   Physical Heart

Entering Orbit

Once the SRBs have shut down and separated for eventual splashdown about 122 nautical miles downrange from the Cape, the shuttle's own engines continue to propel it into successful orbit. *During the next three- to four-week stage of the 90-Day Challenge, you will fine-tune and get more comfortable with the good habits you have established.* Sure, you are still exercising some discipline at this stage, but the "gravitational pull" of those old habits is fading behind you, and you are finding it easier to make healthy heart choices.

At this point, about halfway through the 90-day process, your daily health disciplines will have greater meaning to you because you will be enjoying some of the positive results of your choices. You will sense a closer personal connection with God. Your outlook on life will be much brighter. And you probably will feel better physically and may even weigh a little less. You're going to be so glad you got started when you did and so motivated to continue!

Maintaining Orbit

Once the shuttle enters orbit, the big push is over. The thrusters shut down and the vehicle settles into a predictable orbital pattern at more than 17,000 miles per hour. This doesn't mean there won't be the need for occasional mid-course maneuvers. But at this stage in the mission, just short, strategic bursts from small thrusters can keep the vehicle on course.

During the third stage of the 90-Day Challenge, you will look and feel more like the person you want to be than the person you were. The healthy habits you established are becoming your normal, second-nature way of doing things. You no longer dread exercise; instead, you really miss that 30-minute jog each day when something unexpected cuts into your schedule. You don't think twice about looking for something healthy on the menu instead of automatically ordering a triple-bypass burger. And you actually look forward to enriching your soul each day by reading something from the Bible and talking to God through personal, heartfelt prayer.

Our 90-Day Challenge to You

We firmly believe that three months after embracing our Total Heart Health challenge, you will look into the mirror and see a new man! Why am I so confident? Because a lifestyle transformation has been the joyous experience of a rapidly growing number of men who have taken this challenge to heart, including me.

When you finish this book, the next step is to accept our 90-Day Challenge and begin your personal lifestyle transformation. We will give you the details in the chapters ahead, culminating in chapter 21. And to help you follow through with the challenge, we invite you to enter into a Lifestyle Transformation Commitment. You will find the form on page xv. You may complete the agreement anytime between now and the day you launch your personal 90-Day Challenge.

My writing partners and I have found that any significant change in our lives requires a serious commitment to change. Signing a commitment helps us follow through with the intentions of our hearts. That's why we encourage you to do so. Please note that signing your name on the Lifestyle Transformation Commitment expresses your *intention* to change. You may not reach all your goals or fulfill all your hopes, but your serious commitment will head you in the right direction. Making your commitment in writing will provide added momentum for you to complete the challenge.

Our approach to the disciplines of a healthy heart may seem legalistic to some. But there's a big difference between legalism and discipline. A legalist will try to follow every rule, hoping to please the people he looks up to, including God. A disciplined person will exert every effort and make sacrifices to reach his desired goals. Legalism is not a healthy lifestyle, but discipline is. Discipline and self-control go hand in hand. No one can make a lifestyle change without exercising discipline, and that's what our plan will help you do.

Now let's get ready for ignition and liftoff. In part 1, we will explore the unique nature of a man's total heart and why it is so important to pursue Total Heart Health. In part 2, we will confront the deadly enemies of a man's heart, those forces that can rob you of your health and even your life. And in part 3, we will look at numerous strategies for nurturing your total heart to steadily improve your total health.

Are you buckled in? Then let's hit the throttle.

Keys to Total Heart Health

Introduction: Man to Man, Heart to Heart

- To enjoy Total Heart Health, you must take care of the heart in its totality—spiritual and physical.
- Getting into a Total Heart Health lifestyle takes about 90 days.
- The first three weeks of the Total Heart Health plan will help you soar free of destructive old habits and replace them with healthy new habits.
- During the next three- to four-week stage of the 90-Day Challenge, you will fine-tune and get more comfortable with the good habits you've established.
- During the third stage of the 90-Day Challenge, you will look and feel more like the person you want to be than the person you were.
- No one can make a lifestyle change without exercising discipline, and that's what the 90-Day Challenge will help you do.

Total Heart Health
Lifestyle Transformation Commitment

1. Your Personal Information

Name _____ Age _____

My present weight is _____.

My present body mass index (see chapter 7) is _____.

My present blood pressure is _____.

I presently spend _____ minutes per day in some form of exercise.

I presently spend _____ minutes per day in Bible reading and prayer.

2. Your Goals

In general terms, what do you want to accomplish by taking the 90-Day Total Heart Health Challenge?

_____

_____

_____

In 90 days . . .

I want my weight to be _____.

I want my body mass index to be _____.

I want my blood pressure to be _____.

I want to be spending 30 minutes per day exercising.

I want to be spending 30 minutes per day in Bible reading and prayer.

3. Your Commitment

Seal your agreement in prayer to God. You may want to pray the following prayer or use it as a pattern for your own prayer.

Dear God, thank You for the heart You have given me. I now commit to pursuing Total Heart Health for the next 90 days. Give me the discipline and encouragement to live out my commitment. Develop in me a new lifestyle that will bring greater health to my total heart so I may fulfill the purposes for which You put me in the world. In Jesus's name, amen.

Your signature _____

Date _____

Part 1

The Dynamic Qualities
of a Man's Heart

1

You Gotta Have Heart—Total Heart

A real man is all heart, not just a collection
of important parts.

Dr. Ed Young

Do you know any guys like Reuben? Rueben is a thirty-something who spends many hours a week at a gym pumping iron to sculpt a physique like the ones in those commercials for bodybuilding machines. And his arteries are just as lean as his abs. He hasn't so much as sniffed a bag of French fries or a Twinkie in more than six years. The problem is, the gym and the health-food store are his world. His closest relationships are with his workout buddies, and all they talk about is working out. Reuben could wear out a fleet of treadmills and never have a heart attack. But he is not as heart healthy as his body-fat numbers would indicate.

Maybe you work with a mover and shaker like Wayne. He's not climbing the corporate ladder; he's on an express elevator to the corner office. He puts in fourteen-hour days at the office and still spends two to three hours a night on the laptop at home. His goal is to make vice president before he's forty. In the meantime, Wayne drinks too much and scoffs at physical fitness. He has little time or interest in lesser endeavors, such as saving his marriage or investigating God's claims on his life. Wayne may win the vice president's office by the time he's forty, but the way he's mistreating his heart, he could just as easily end up in a hospital room or a viewing room.

There may also be a Russell among your acquaintances. Russell, in his fifties, is all heart, at least that's what most people say. He's a deacon in the church and spends many hours every week helping people in need. But this good-hearted deacon is about to be fired from his third job in four years.

Russell has a history of showing up for work late and leaving early. And he keeps putting off a physical exam, despite his wife's insistence that he go. He hasn't felt right for months, but he's too busy getting good things done to worry about it. All things considered, Russell's big heart may not be as big as people think.

Then there's the Alan in many of our lives. This guy is young, unattached, and making plenty of money. But Alan's life really revolves around sports and having fun. He's got all the toys: an entertainment system that can blow out windows, access to a gazillion cable sports channels, and a collection of rare sports memorabilia that he will retire on someday. Alan has dated a lot of young women, but they lose interest once they realize they always will play second string to Alan's sports heroes.

Where Are the Stout-Hearted Men These Days?

Don't you think there's a little bit of these four men in all of us? Life is so full of important, meaningful, and enjoyable experiences that we can't seem to make them all fit together. We feel fragmented, out of balance, pulled in so many directions that we have difficulty doing justice to anything. We all want to excel in our jobs, stay reasonably fit, accomplish some good with our lives, and have some fun along the way. But it doesn't seem there are enough hours in the day, and we don't have the energy for all we need to do and want to do. So our hearts are divided, and some things—including important things—sometimes draw the short straw.

Segmented, unbalanced lives are all too common among men today. But it doesn't have to be this way, nor should it be. You are not a collection of parts that operate independently of one another. God created you to be a whole man with many closely integrated facets, such as body, mind, emotions, and relationships. These areas are all interrelated and cannot be parceled out into categories of success or failure. When one area of your life is neglected or stressed, the whole person suffers as a result.

In his lyrics, Oscar Hammerstein II popularized the phrase "stout-hearted men." According to the song, stout-hearted men act on their dreams to make them real and their hearts inspire other men with their fire. Mike, Rick, and

I believe that real stout-hearted men are wholehearted men. Wholehearted men are the ones who have the best opportunity to live out their dreams and inspire others with their fire. When it comes to a man's heart, a total heart is greater than the sum of its parts. We believe God designed men to experience wholeness and health in body, soul, and spirit.

Looking at the caricatures of the four men described above may remind you of areas where you would like to enjoy greater health physically, spiritually, emotionally, or relationally. You may want to lose a few pounds and strengthen that physical heart of yours with a more disciplined exercise regimen. Maybe you yearn to draw closer to God and invite Him to be more involved in your daily life. Or perhaps you long for your life to come together in all areas, to feel that your heart is whole, together, and heading in the right direction. If so, this book is for you.

Whatever your heart goals may be, we confidently make this promise to you: if you will devote about one hour a day to Total Heart Health for 90 days straight—roughly thirty minutes to strengthening your physical heart and thirty minutes to strengthening your spiritual heart, while eating sensibly in the process—your life will be changed. You will begin to enjoy benefits that will last you a lifetime.

Components of a Wholehearted Man

When it comes to your heart, there's more to you than meets the eye. Let me take a minute to reacquaint you with the two major components of a wholehearted man.

The Ticker That Keeps on Ticking

Throughout this book, Mike Duncan and Rick Leachman will tell you about the wonders of your physical heart and the importance of keeping it healthy. But allow me to give you a quick overview of your heart in layman's terms.

Make a fist with one of your hands, right there where you're sitting; then take a good look at it. Located somewhere behind your ribs in the middle of your chest, your heart is about the size of that fist. Every minute of your life, at least a gallon and a half of your blood is pumped through your heart. And when you're jogging on the track or the treadmill or playing a furious game of racquetball, it can pump up to eight gallons per minute through about sixty thousand miles of arteries, veins, and capillaries. Amazing!

You may have been told that your heart keeps up this pace for a lifetime without any rest. Technically, that's not true. You've heard a human heartbeat amplified, haven't you—if not your own, perhaps the heartbeat of a loved one? To me it sounds like the heart is saying, *Loved up, loved up, loved up, loved up*—which is a good thing for a heart to say. But between every *up* and the next *loved* is a pause that's about twice as long as the beat. God masterfully designed your heart with a built-in R&R feature. It rests and relaxes between every single beat. No wonder it can keep ticking for eighty, ninety, one hundred years or more.

I believe God's design for the heart tells us something about His design for the rhythm of our lives. We need to rest and relax twice as long as we work. And isn't it interesting that the common workday is about eight hours and that we use about twice that amount for sleep and recreation? When people stray from God's rhythm for work and rest—I'm talking about workaholics here—they add undue stress to their hearts, and that can lead to all kinds of physical problems.

Here's another fascinating fact about your physical heart. It has a built-in pacemaker that keeps it ticking like a watch connected to a hundred-year battery. About seventy to eighty times every minute, an electrochemical charge sweeps over your heart, and it beats in response to this charge—*loved up, loved up, loved up*. Even more interesting, this pacemaker of yours is self-generating. You cut the nerves to your legs, and they won't move. You cut the nerves to your lungs, and you stop breathing. But if you cut the nerves to the heart's pacemaker, it will keep on zapping the heart with that vital electrochemical charge. Borrowing the words from an old Timex watch commercial, your heart can take a licking and keep on ticking.

As magnificent and efficient as your heart is, your heart isn't what keeps you alive. It's what your heart delivers to the cells of your body that keeps you humming along: your blood and all the nutrients you need. William Harvey, English court physician to King James I and King Charles I, discovered the circulatory system in the early 1600s. That's when he declared to the world his revolutionary and, at that time, controversial discovery: it is the blood circulating through the body that gives life. Had the medical community paid closer attention to the Bible, they would have recognized this truth millennia sooner. In Leviticus 17:11, God told the Israelites, "The life of the flesh is in the blood."

Not long ago, I talked with someone who had witnessed kidney-transplant surgery. This person said that when the transplant team brought in the donated kidney, it looked pale and anemic—like a piece of meat that had gone bad. But once they put the kidney in place and the patient's blood began to flow through it, the organ turned red and vibrant. The life of that kidney was in the blood that pulsed through it.

Of course, your blood would be of no help to you at all if your heart didn't do its job. That's why taking care of your physical heart is literally a matter of life and death. Keep your heart free from disease, and it will keep you alive. Disregard the principles for heart health, and you run the risk of shearing years off your life and bringing tragedy to your loved ones.

The two obvious keys to keeping your ticker ticking strongly are diet and exercise. You just can't go through life on the run eating whatever is convenient and quick. If you want a healthy heart and a long life, you must be thoughtful and purposeful about your diet. We're not saying you have to give up juicy steaks and sugary desserts for life. That's no way to live either. You just have to be smart about what and how much you eat. In part 3, Drs. Duncan and Leachman will share with you sensible, healthy, and realistic nutrition tips that include foods you already enjoy.

As for exercise, you cannot assume that just because you live an active life, you get the exercise you really need for a healthy heart. Your physical workouts each week must be intentional, scheduled, and aimed at specific health goals. A good exercise plan will provide moderate exertion several times a week. And if you think exercise is boring, our physical heart health team has a pleasant surprise in store for you. Exercising your heart to better health can be fun!

The Heart That Cannot Be Transplanted

Just as a healthy physical heart keeps your body well, so a healthy spiritual heart is essential to keeping the rest of you well. Wise King Solomon wrote,

"Keep vigilant watch over your heart; *that's* where life starts" (Proverbs 4:23 MSG). The spiritual heart is mentioned more than eight hundred times in the Bible. It's the spiritual heart we're talking about when we use words like *heartfelt, tender-hearted, hardhearted*, and *heartbreaking*. It's this heart we mean when we say, "My heart was touched," "My heart goes out to him," "God spoke to my heart," "He has a lot of heart," and "I'm sick at heart about it."

Flowing from the vital life center of the spiritual heart are our passions, our desires, our dreams, our characters, and our choices. Everyone can put on an act for a while. We can behave the way we know we should, say the right thing at the right time, and be the person others expect us to be. But eventually what's in our hearts is going to flow out. If the heart is not healthy, in time it will show up in our words, speech, decisions, responses, and reactions. That's why we must guard our hearts vigilantly. A healthy spiritual heart is essential to a healthy spiritual life.

Unless you guard your heart, unless you pursue a healthy spiritual heart as well as a healthy physical heart, you will be vulnerable to life-crippling spiritual heart disease. How can you guard your heart? You let God go to work on it with His Word. There are at least three ways the Bible can keep your spiritual heart healthy.

The Word of God makes precise, lifesaving incisions like a surgeon's scalpel. Hebrews 4:12–14 says, "His powerful Word is sharp as a surgeon's scalpel, cutting through everything, whether doubt or defense, laying us open to listen and obey. Nothing and no one is impervious to God's Word. We can't get away from it—no matter what" (MSG).

We all need spiritual heart surgery from time to time for strengthening weak muscles and cutting away diseased tissue. You need God's precise, healing Word in the hands of the Master Surgeon to keep your heart healthy and growing strong.

God's Word purifies and cauterizes like a flame. The Lord spoke through the Old Testament prophet Jeremiah, "Is not My word like fire?" (Jeremiah 23:29). It's so easy to surround our hearts with rationalizations about what is right, what is good, and what we should do. Our human way of doing things tries to cut a deal with God based on our best ideas and plans. Isn't that the height of arrogance to try to tell God what to do? That's when we need the purifying, healing fire of the Word to burn away what is extraneous, that humanistic spin we tend to put on life.

God is so deeply concerned for the health of our hearts that He will sometimes resort to force. Still speaking through Jeremiah, the Lord continues, "Is not My word . . . like a hammer which shatters a rock?" (v. 29). Sometimes we are so hardhearted that God needs to allow difficult circumstances in our lives in order to turn our attention to His Word for solutions.

When a person needs open-heart surgery, the surgeon must inflict some damage and pain in order to get inside the rib cage and heal the heart. If he doesn't cut into the chest cavity, the disease can't be cured. His intent is not to be malicious or hurtful; he only wants to heal and nurture your heart to wholeness.

Your Spiritual Heart Health Depends on You

The success of God's heart-healing work depends on an active response from you, just as maintaining a healthy physical heart requires you to be proactive with diet and exercise.

You will encourage spiritual heart health by maintaining a consistent personal connection with God. Follow a daily plan that includes setting aside time to pray and read something from the Bible. We will talk more about going one-on-one with God later in this book.

Staying healthy spiritually and physically is aided by being in church. Many surveys have shown a positive link between church attendance and physical health. One study conducted by Robert Hummer of the University of Texas surveyed twenty-one thousand adults for a nine-year period. People who never attend church, the survey revealed, "are four times as likely to die from respiratory disease, diabetes, or infectious diseases."[1] When you are active in church, you are doing yourself and your health a huge favor!

Spiritual heart health is an ongoing discipline, just as physical heart health is. Interspersed between the insights on physical heart health from our two doctors, we will share helpful tips for keeping your spiritual heart strong and healthy.

Living Wholeheartedly

When I think of a man's journey toward Total Heart Health, King David comes to mind. He prayed, "Put me together, one heart and mind; then, undivided, I'll worship in joyful fear" (Psalm 86:11 MSG). David knew about the segmented life, the fragmented heart, and all the pain that goes with it. He cried out to God, asking Him to pull all the pieces together so his total heart would be centered on God.

That's a great prayer, isn't it? "Lord, give me a whole heart focused on You." When you ask God for an undivided heart, get ready. That's just what He loves to do. As you get on the road toward living wholeheartedly, here are four keys to keep in mind.

Your Physical Heart and Your Spiritual Heart Are "Joined at the Hip"

In the Bible, the creation account says, "The LORD God formed man of dust from the ground." That's the material, physical part of us, but God wasn't finished. The verse continues, "and breathed into his nostrils the breath of life; and man became a living being" (Genesis 2:7). "Being" in this verse literally means "soul." That's the immaterial, spiritual part of us—our thoughts, feelings, motives, choices, desires, fears, hopes, ideas, dreams, purposes, guilts, joys, and so on.

God created us as physical *and* spiritual beings, and whatever happens to one part affects the other. No wonder the apostle Paul prayed, "May God himself, the God who makes everything holy and whole . . . put you together—spirit, soul, and body—and keep you fit for the coming of our Master, Jesus Christ" (1 Thessalonians 5:23 MSG).

God wants you to grow in health as a whole person. Physical heart health and spiritual heart health are tightly interlocked.

Getting Your Heart in Shape Is a Process

You and a bunch of guys gather at a friend's house on a fall Saturday afternoon to watch the big game on a big-screem TV. At halftime, somebody suggests a game of driveway hoops. You start strong, but after only five minutes you head for the sidelines sucking wind. You're so far out of shape it's not funny. Did it happen overnight? Of course not. You've been losing "shape" ever since you got lazy about working out. And that spare tire around your middle didn't appear while you were asleep either. It's been growing on you for months.

Getting out of shape physically and spiritually happens over a period of weeks and months, so getting back in shape will take time too. In the pages ahead, we will encourage you and coach you in the process of developing healthy heart patterns on the road to Total Heart Health—body and soul. This is no fad program guaranteeing instant success. It's an ongoing process in which every small step takes you farther from where you've been and nearer to where you want to be.

Total Heart Health Is Always About Two Hearts in Sync

As a young man, I dreamed of building bridges, so I enrolled at the University of Alabama to become an engineer. But as a freshman, my belief in God was challenged by an atheist, so I launched into a serious search for God's purpose for my life. Six months later, I committed my life to being a pastor, and I've been at it ever since. In my chapters, I will share with you biblical principles and strategies to help you grow a healthy spiritual heart.

You will strengthen your physical heart as you take care to exercise each day and maintain a healthy diet. Mike Duncan and Rick Leachman will be the point men on the physical heart track. They have extensive clinical experience and insight into men's heart health. They will share with you from their vast knowledge and expertise how to pursue and achieve physical heart health.

As you pursue these two tracks simultaneously, beginning with the 90-Day Challenge, your total heart will grow strong and remain strong.

Total Heart Health Is Not a Passing Fad but a Lifelong Pursuit

The Bible teaches, paradoxically, that the total health of your spiritual heart will not be realized until your physical heart stops beating. For the Christian, death is the doorway into the fullness of life. So our spiritual heart health is always in process until we enter God's presence in heaven. As long as you pursue a deeper, more intimate relationship with God and His Word, your spiritual heart will improve in health.

As for your physical heart, you can look forward to a process of improving heart health over time—up to a point. But inevitably, age and perhaps disease or injury will weaken your heart, and it will stop beating for good. But in the meantime, you can and should pursue optimum heart health, both to extend and to enjoy the decades ahead.

This side of heaven, there is no point at which you can say, "I have arrived. My heart is totally healthy." There are always additional steps to take on this journey in order to maintain the level of heart health you have achieved and to lift your health to the next level. And every step you take is a positive step in the direction of Total Heart Health.

It's time to narrow our focus on that heart of yours. Mike Duncan and Rick Leachman will now get you up to speed on the characteristics of a man's physical heart and the ways it is different from a woman's heart.

Keys to Total Heart Health

Chapter 1: You Gotta Have Heart—Total Heart

- Segmented, unbalanced lives are all too common among men today.

- God created you to be a whole man with many closely integrated facets, and when one area of your life is neglected or stressed, the whole person suffers as a result.

- God designed men to experience wholeness and health in body, soul, and spirit.

- God's design for the heart tells us something about the design for the rhythm of our lives: we need to rest and relax twice as long as we work.

- The two obvious keys to keeping your ticker ticking strongly are diet and exercise.

- Just as a healthy physical heart keeps your body well, so a healthy spiritual heart is essential to keeping the rest of you well.

- There are at least three ways the Bible can keep your spiritual heart healthy: it makes precise, lifesaving incisions like a surgeon's scalpel; it purifies and cauterizes like a flame; and it is sometimes an instrument of force.

- There are four keys to wholehearted living:
    1. Your physical and spiritual hearts are linked.
    2. Getting your heart in shape is a process.
    3. Total Heart Health is always about two hearts in sync.
    4. Total Heart Health is not a passing fad but a lifelong pursuit.

2
The Unique Nature
of a Man's Physical Heart

Getting up close and personal with the blood pump that keeps you alive.

Dr. Michael Duncan and Dr. Richard Leachman

A man was walking into the hospital for an appointment when he noticed two doctors in lab coats searching through the flower beds near the entrance.

"Excuse me," the man said, "have you lost something?"

"No," replied one of the doctors. "We're about to perform a heart transplant on a tax auditor, and we're looking for the right-sized stone."

This old joke has a lot of miles on it, and it has been used to poke fun at many people we sometimes perceive as hardhearted. But in reality, there is no substitute for a healthy human heart. Perhaps medical technology will one day perfect a mechanical heart that's as efficient and dependable as the human heart. But until that day, you'll do well to take care of the original equipment God gave you to keep you alive.

What's So Special About a Man's Heart?

Your fist-sized heart weighs seven to fifteen ounces, depending on your overall body weight, and is roughly cone-shaped with the smaller end at the bottom. The human heart is made up of muscle tissue and is hollow so it can serve as a temporary reservoir for blood. The heart's function during your lifetime is to keep your blood circulating through the arteries, veins, and capillaries of your body. If you achieve the normal life expectancy of

15

around seventy-four years for men, your heart will beat about 3.5 billion times.

A man's heart is generally larger than a woman's heart, simply because men on average are larger than women in overall body size. Compare your fist with a woman's fist to get an idea of the heart size difference. But there are other physical characteristics related to the heart that set men apart from women. It is important for you to understand these differences, because they have an impact on your heart health.

A Man Has a Higher Metabolic Rate

Stacy and Mick are on a diet. They carefully watch what they eat and run three miles a day together. But Mick is losing more weight than Stacy, and it irritates her to no end. There's good reason for it, however. A man's internal "engine" for processing calories runs at a faster speed than a woman's. Bottom line: the average man can eat a little more and exercise a little less than the average woman to achieve the same weight goals and overall health.

A Man's Cholesterol Is Different

Cholesterol is a significant concern in the pursuit of heart health because abnormal cholesterol levels in the blood are known to contribute to heart disease. There are two designations of cholesterol: high-density lipoprotein (HDL) and low-density lipoprotein (LDL). Most people know them as "good" cholesterol (HDL) and "bad" cholesterol (LDL). You may remember that high HDL scores are good and low LDL scores are good.

As a man, you are at a slight genetic disadvantage when it comes to cholesterol. Men tend to have lower levels of good cholesterol than women. So you definitely cannot ignore the concerns about cholesterol in your diet. A woman's advantage in this area goes away later in life. After menopause, decreasing levels of estrogen in a woman's system result in decreasing levels of HDL, meaning that a woman's cholesterol profile after menopause begins to look more like a man's. This change in profile also elevates the risk of heart problems in postmenopausal women. If your wife, mother, or another female loved one is in this age range, encourage them to go in for regular cholesterol screenings.

A Man's Symptoms of Heart Attack and Other Heart Problems Are Different

Generally speaking, heart-attack symptoms in men are more specific than those in women. Typically, we find that men experiencing a heart attack complain of chest discomfort and numbness in the left arm. Shortness of breath and sweating may also occur. However, many men have atypical symptoms, and some may even have a heart attack with no symptoms at all. In fact, it has been estimated that 50 percent of all people with coronary heart disease have as their first event either a heart attack or sudden death. This is why coronary artery disease (CAD) is called the "silent killer."

While some women experience the same symptoms as men, others experience pain at the top of the back, a burning sensation in the upper abdomen, nausea, flulike symptoms, anxiety, and sweating. Some women who suffer a heart attack don't even know it. A man's telltale signs of chest pain and numbness are usually hard to miss or ignore.

Heart Disease in Men Usually Surfaces Earlier in Life

A woman's hormonal makeup works in favor early in life. Estrogen is known to act as a type of shield against cardiovascular disease. After menopause, when estrogen levels decline markedly, is when most women show signs of heart problems. Men, however, do not enjoy the advantage of this estrogen shield. Therefore, men are more susceptible to heart disease throughout life. We have set apart chapter 5 for a thorough exploration of heart disease in men.

A Man's Psychological Approach to Heart Health and Weight Loss Is Different

There are many factors that motivate persons to control their weight and pursue a healthy lifestyle. Men seem primarily motivated by increasing their *strength*, while women pursue these goals to enhance their *appearance*. While both qualities are desirable to both sexes, men tend to stay with diet and exercise to develop muscle, while women do so to look good.

The Seasons of a Man's Heart

God fashioned your physical heart to last for a long, long time. It has a lifetime warranty! But like any product with a good warranty, there are conditions.

As long as you follow the "manufacturer's guidelines," your heart will work hard to keep you healthy. Here's a look at a man's heart through the decades and some important tips for keeping it strong.

The Twenties: Gentlemen, Start Your Engines

Life really gets on track for men in their twenties. Education completed, many launch into a career, some marry and start a family, and most live away from parental control—sometimes *far* away. But without some attention to self-discipline, a man's life of independence and adventure can easily get off-track before it gets very far. A successful career demands hard work within the framework of superiors and corporate goals. A healthy marriage and family require a man's devotion and compassion to those dearest to him. And achieving financial goals is impossible without paying careful attention to budgeting and spending. Lack of focus, discipline, and drive at this stage can ruin everything a man hopes to achieve and enjoy.

This first decade of adulthood is the time to set productive lifestyle patterns. The twenties is the time to establish good heart health habits that will benefit you for the rest of your life. As a growing teenager, you could get by without paying close attention to what you ate. But when the growing years are over, maintaining normal weight for your height means eating healthy foods and getting sufficient exercise. Resist the temptation to eat only what is convenient and cheap. Learn to eat meals that are nutritious and well balanced, keeping the total number of calories low. It can be done—even on a limited budget.

Join a gym, participate in sports leagues at the local community center, or invest in free weights or an exercise machine of some kind. If you can't afford these exercise options, get into running, walking, or doing push-ups, sit-ups, crunches, and so on. Chapter 15 will give you sound advice on how to put together a personal exercise program.

Along with diet and exercise, consult your physician to make sure you are getting sufficient quantities of vitamins and minerals in your diet. In chapters 12 and 13 we will explore more fully the diet and dietary supplements important to men at all life stages. Start your life healthy, and you will likely stay healthy. *Your twenties is the best time in your life to launch into a Total Heart Health lifestyle!*

The most important decision you can make for your heart at this stage is to not smoke—or to stop smoking if you got into it as a teenager. Smoking is a heart killer.

The Thirties: Jockeying for Position

Increasing responsibilities in career and/or family life at this stage of life can be taxing. It may take some creative planning to maintain a Total Heart Health lifestyle through your thirties. Investing long hours in the pursuit of career goals and financial rewards, you may find it difficult to carve out time for physical exercise. Don't go soft on your running, workouts, or sports activities, even if you have to wake up a little earlier or hit the gym during lunch hour.

Healthy eating habits may be tested in the midst of a busy life. You may be tempted to skip breakfast, grab a quick lunch (instead of a healthy lunch), snack too much, and eat too much at dinner. It is important during your thirties to maintain healthy eating habits and, if you're married, to pass those habits along to your family. Your kids may not believe it at first, but prove to them that healthy meals served at the family dinner table can actually taste good! In the process, use this time to teach them about good nutrition.

Often during this decade, hypertension (high blood pressure) and lipid (cholesterol) abnormalities begin to manifest themselves. It's important to schedule regular checkups with your doctor so any problems can be diagnosed early and treated.

The Forties: Battling for the Lead

Most men in their forties are fully involved—and sometimes overinvolved—in career pursuits. This is the decade when some men begin to put on weight. Increased earnings and a higher standard of living often accompany career success at this stage. And with more discretionary income comes the temptation to eat richer foods and dine out more often, resulting in greater calorie intake. Some men eat more at this stage in response to job stress and life pressures.

Also, as energy begins to wane, forty-something men may become lax when it comes to exercise, resulting in fewer calories burned. More calories taken in coupled with fewer calories worked out equals weight gain. Disciplined diet and exercise are a must at this stage to avoid unwanted pounds.

Important note: any signs of high blood pressure or cholesterol problems must be treated aggressively with medication. This is also the time for your doctor to check for the presence of latent diabetes, especially if you are overweight.

The Fifties: Lapping the Competition

After twenty to thirty years of hard work, many of a man's long-term career and financial goals are within sight in the decade of his fifties. By this time he may have more subordinates than superiors in the workplace and enjoy greater control over his schedule and responsibilities on the job. As a result, he may have more time flexibility for maintaining a workout routine. This is the decade when some men finally decide to do something about the "spare tire," the low energy level, and high blood pressure. Many guys at this stage lament, "I wish I'd been more disciplined about staying at my college weight."

This is the decade when many married couples ride an emotional roller coaster. For those who started families in their twenties, the kids are grown and leaving home for college, marriage, and career. Those couples who delayed parenting until midlife may still have children at home, but the empty nest is within sight. Let's be honest here: as much as we want our children to move into adulthood, it's not easy—and sometimes it's downright tough—to see our young ones leave the nest. Furthermore, when the children leave home and Dad and Mom are alone again, a couple may learn that they have less in common. It can be a crisis point for many marriages.

Even though it may be a time of sadness, the season of the empty nest is also a time for taking on tasks you have put off through the busy childrearing years. It's a time when many husbands and wives rediscover the romance and fun that sometimes get buried under an avalanche of career building and kids' sports and school programs. It's a time to get serious about the plans, dreams, vacations, and hobbies you just didn't have time for while the kids were still at home. And with education expenses reduced, now's the time to get that fitness club membership you always wanted.

The Sixties and Beyond: Turning Toward the Checkered Flag

Some men have the luxury at this stage of choosing between continued advancement in their chosen field, an exciting second career, retirement, or semiretirement. But this is not the time to pull the plug on healthy heart pursuits. It is important to keep exercising. You probably won't be able to crank the treadmill up to top speed like you did as a young buck, but the good news is you don't need to. Just maintain an active life as much as possible and spend at least thirty minutes a day six days a week in some form of purposeful exercise: walking or jogging (on the treadmill, in the neighborhood, or on a local track), playing a sport such as tennis or golf, or working out on a resistance machine set to accommodate your level of strength.

No matter what decade you find yourself in, physical heart health is both important and achievable. Don't allow the duties and demands of these normal life stages to rob your heart of the care it deserves. Whether you're a single twenty-something or a grandfather, now is the time to establish a healthy heart lifestyle. We encourage you to begin your journey with the 90-Day Challenge summarized in chapter 19.

A man's spiritual heart is as unique and special as his physical heart. Dr. Ed Young will now tell you why.

Keys to Total Heart Health

Chapter 2: The Unique Nature of a Man's Physical Heart

- A man's heart is different from a woman's heart. It is generally larger, a man has a higher metabolic rate, his cholesterol is different, his heart attack symptoms are different, heart disease surfaces in the male earlier in life, and his psychological approach to heart health and weight loss is different.

- The twenties, the first decade of adulthood, is the time when a man should set productive lifestyle patterns.

- In their thirties, men may see abnormalities beginning to manifest, such as high blood pressure and high cholesterol. It's important for men in their thirties to begin having regular checkups with their doctors.

- In their forties, men often begin to put on weight and get lax in exercise. This is also the time for your doctor to check for latent diabetes, especially if you're overweight.

- In their fifties, many men decide it's time to do something about the "spare tire," low energy level, and high blood pressure.

- In their sixties and beyond, men must not stop exercising and eating a healthy diet, because physical heart health is important and achievable in every season of a man's life.

3

The Unique Nature
of a Man's Spiritual Heart

You see God differently than a woman does, so deal with
Him like a man.

Dr. Ed Young

Several years ago, actress and comedienne Julia Sweeney, then a cast member on
Saturday Night Live, gained TV fame for her androgynous character, "Pat."
Sweeney purposely wore costumes and makeup that made it impossible to tell if
Pat was a man or a woman. Even the nickname Pat was intended to contribute
to the ambivalence. In each skit, other characters tried to figure out if Pat was
male or female by asking her leading questions. And the naive Pat always came
up with a viable answer that left the truth in doubt, which made for great laughs.

Androgynous means having the characteristics of both a man and a woman.
Think of those times you've seen a person in the mall or somewhere and wondered, *Hmm, is that a he or a she?* Sometimes it's hard to tell. Androgyny is a
human invention. God designed men and women to be two distinct genders,
wonderful and unique in their own ways. One of the ways to keep your spiritual heart healthy is to affirm the man God made you to be and relate to Him
just as you are.

Vive la Différence!

Men and women are comprised of spirit, soul, and body, but that's about where
the similarity ends. As someone quipped, "Men and women are made of the
same basic materials; women are just put together better." And all the guys
said, "Amen!" As a man, you obviously are built and wired differently from a

woman. Let's review some of these differences and see how they impact your relationship with God.

You're Physically Unique

Unless you're looking at someone like Pat, the physical differences between men and women are quite obvious and notable. As the doctors have mentioned, men are typically larger than women, and with the larger body size comes greater physical strength. I've heard it said that men are on average 10 percent taller than women, 20 percent heavier, and have 30 percent greater strength, especially in the upper body. So you're not likely to see a woman playing tackle or guard on an NFL team. But in other sports where physical skill is more important than size and strength—such as tennis or golf—you may find some women more accomplished than men.

Not too many generations ago, these physical differences meant a great deal to society. Providing for a family involved a lot more physical labor than it does today, so men did the hard work of hunting, plowing, harvesting, building a home, and so on. Industrialization introduced laborsaving machinery that women could operate. So today, we find women in many occupations where brute physical strength is no longer a prime requirement.

What do a man's unique physical traits have to do with his spiritual heart? I believe God has created us men to protect and serve those who are not as strong as we are—whether they are men, women, or children. So whenever you move furniture for your elderly parents, build new cabinets for your wife's craft room, reach something on a high shelf for a small child, install a water heater for your girlfriend, or perform any heavy task for someone in need, you are fulfilling the roll of strength for which God has uniquely equipped you as a man. And your service to others in God's strength becomes heart-strengthening worship to God.

You're Emotionally Unique

Somebody has joked that the emotional difference between men and women is that men are crabby all month long. I hope that's not true. Yet men and women are wired differently emotionally, and research has shown that our wiring has everything to do with how we respond to situations.

For example, when little boys come up against obstacles, they tend to push them out of the way, while girls tend to go around them. Who taught boys and girls to handle obstacles differently? Nobody. It's in the way God made them. Studies have shown that when a six-month-old girl hears jazz music playing, her heartbeat increases. But when a six-month-old boy hears jazz, he shows absolutely no physical response at all. How did they learn these different responses at such a tender age? They didn't learn the responses; it's the way God wired them.

Psychologists tell us that men equate maturity with *independence,* while women view maturity in terms of *interdependence.* A man is out to make his mark in the world, whether it be in a career, a mission, or a hobby. These pursuits often take him away from his wife, family, or friends for great periods of time. But a woman is likely driven more by togetherness with others in her life. You may love working long hours hammering out business deals. But somewhere there is a woman—your wife or girlfriend, your mother, your sister, your daughter—who wishes you were spending some of that time with her. You can't wait until hunting season starts to get out and bag that elusive deer. But the woman in your life can't wait until the season ends so you can get back to attending the symphony with her.

The way you are is the product of an inner mechanism, the makeup of your soul, your emotions, your very heart. Independence and interdependence are both God-given qualities. Men are generally more gifted at independence; women are more gifted at interdependence. Neither is wrong, though they can be expressed in wrong ways. For example, a man may be so driven to establish his independence in business or sport that he neglects the women in his life. You can strengthen your spiritual heart by making room in your life for others even in those times when you would rather hole up with your work or your hobby.

You're Spiritually Unique

Men are also wired differently in how they relate to God. If you don't believe it, consider how a men's spiritual retreat differs from a women's retreat.

Here's how the women do it. Laura, a member of the women's ministry staff at our church, says she would go with a retreat theme drawn from current events but shaped for a spiritual retreat. "Extreme Makeover" is an idea Laura likes. She would invite speakers and arrange breakout sessions on makeover topics like cosmetics and hairstyles while challenging women to welcome the makeover of spirit, mind, and emotions. The program would carve out time for women to sit together in small groups with coffee and talk about their problems and needs.

Sound interesting to you? I didn't think so. But there's more.

Laura would select a comfortable retreat center not far from a mall or town so ladies could enjoy shopping during free time. Great attention and expense would be focused on motif and decorations, including platform appearance, table decorations, centerpieces, and even gift baskets waiting in the guests' rooms. The menu would feature healthy gourmet meals. Laura would also arrange for after-school childcare so moms could leave for the retreat on Friday afternoon.

Roger is a pastor and a former professional golfer who once hosted a TV show on hunting and fishing. Here's his idea of a spiritual retreat for men.

Roger would focus on themes like integrity, loyalty, and leadership qualities. His guest speakers would be drawn from the ranks of coaches, military leaders, Christian business leaders, and political activists. The retreat site would be somewhere in the country, the more rustic the better, and the menu would center on mass quantities of anything that can be served with cream gravy. Decorations would take a backseat to a high-powered sound system, a PowerPoint setup, and a monstrous TV for watching football on Saturday afternoon. Other free-time activities would include target shooting, basketball, a golf tournament, and fishing.

Sounds like a great retreat to me! How about you?

When it comes to a man's spiritual heart, there are at least four ways in which God has wired you differently from a woman.

Men seek heroic faith. While a woman's spiritual heart is wired to respond especially to God's tenderness, a man's heart is spiritually attuned to God's toughness, strength, and heroic stature.

In 2004, California governor Arnold Schwarzenegger borrowed a phrase from TV comedy when he called opponents of his economic reform proposals "girlie men." Another faddish term used in the twenty-first century is "metrosexual." The two ideas describe men who morph into a form somewhere between male and female in style and behavior. Not all "girlie men" or "metrosexuals" are androgynous or homosexual, but all favor more of their "feminine side."

The characters in the popular TV series *Frasier* illustrated this kind of man. Frasier and his brother, Niles, loved coffee bars and quiche and relished the thought of going to a male spa. Niles got excited about seasoning crepe pans. If Martin, their father, invited his sons to a basketball game, they shrank in horror, preferring the symphony. Yet they were thoroughly heterosexual, as evidenced by their serial sexual relationships with women.

The therapeutic society took root in the late twentieth century as we were encouraged by the culture to "get in touch" with our emotions. This trend encouraged churches to adopt a touchy-feely religious style. The emphasis on sin, repentance, objective truth, and defined doctrine gave way to relativism and emotionalism. People no longer talked; they "shared." Men were pressed into small groups where they were urged to "open up," which usually meant participating in a teary, soul-baring, tell-all more characteristic of a sorority gabfest than a men's shoot-the-bull session around a deer carcass and a campfire.

The trend toward neutering the male gender has extended to God. Controversy flared when a popular modern translation of the Bible introduced gender-neutral pronouns to refer to God. Liberal Christianity embraced the idea of God as a "she," and a major denomination's women's conference encouraged worshiping the "goddess."

All this has led to the feminization of Christian faith. No wonder so many guys feel uncomfortable in church. They have difficulty singing drippy, cabaret-style songs in a worship service. They don't mind giving fellow worshipers a warm handshake or a pat on the back, but they aren't as excited when the leader says, "Let's all give each other a great big hug!"

Many churches have become matriarchies where men feel inferior. So men sit on the sidelines, allowing women to take primary leadership roles, further feminizing the church. Men are not victims in this, because they often shrink back from their biblically mandated leadership responsibility, creating a vacuum.

A man's spiritual heart loves images like the captain of the Lord's host, who appeared to Joshua on the eve of the Jericho battle; the mighty God strengthening David as he faced Goliath; and Jesus standing up to the scribes and Pharisees and overturning the tables of the price-gougers in the temple. The male heart is fired by heroic faith in a God of heroic stature!

Men are less dependent. There's a subtle difference between "independence" and "less dependence." Independence can bring to mind a rugged individualist who doesn't give a hoot about others and their opinions. Less dependence describes a person who appreciates others and their views but doesn't lean on them. Men tend to be less dependent on others than women.

Lee Ann and Stan reveal the difference. Lee Ann is at the church every Tuesday morning for a women's share group. On Thursday night, she likes to attend a neighborhood Bible study where women gather in a home to watch videos featuring a popular female Bible teacher. Stan has a hard time understanding why Lee Ann wants to go to these women's groups so much, but she says she needs her friends.

Stan loves to hunt and can't wait for the season to open. He enjoys going with three or four buddies, but he also likes hanging out alone in a deer blind for hours.

Lee Ann has strengths that Stan doesn't have, such as her greater ability to endure pain. But she also has an innate aversion to exposure and aloneness, translating into the spiritual quality of welcoming the support, protection, and leadership of others. There are times when Stan counts on his wife for emotional support, such as when she notices and comments on his accomplishments. And he loves it when Lee Ann softens and slips into his arms. He needs to feel he's covering and protecting her from outside threats. He appreciates the leadership of his foreman at work and the man who leads his early morning men's Bible study group, but doesn't lean on these guys for emotional support as Lee Ann counts on her girlfriends.

Do you see a bit of yourself in Stan in terms of being less dependent on others than some of the women you know? That's how God made you. Spiritually, this means you need to guard your heart from being too independent, thinking you can go it alone without God and without a couple of guys to keep you honest. You may not need as much affirmation from others to foster a strong spiritual journey because you can find much satisfaction in a deeply personal relationship with God.

Men are more goal-driven. Former New York City mayor Rudolph Giuliani says it's important to align "system with purpose." Women tend to be more system-driven, while men are more purpose- or goal-driven. This is why maintaining the household budget and bill paying often fall to the wife. Women seem to be more adept at keeping the system moving smoothly. The man of the house may take on the task of managing the family's investments because there are goals to be achieved: college education for the kids, building their dream home, retirement.

Looking at it another way, the goal-driven men in the car just want to keep the pedal to the metal and get where they're going. But for the process-driven women in the car, stopping along the way to shop or see the sights together is the best part of the trip.

For men, a problem needs to be fixed. For women, a problem needs to be mulled over and talked through. Men have no problem charging ahead alone to get something done. Women are more likely to share their vision with others and welcome on their journey people who will commiserate with them, counsel them, and keep them company.

This is not to say that men don't understand and appreciate process and women don't pursue and benefit from goals. What's in view here is a general tendency. So when companies plan major relocations, they often look to women to guide the process, since 88 percent of relocation administrators are women, according to one survey.[1] And when President George W. Bush took on the task of toppling the regime of Saddam Hussein, he turned to men like General Tommy Franks just as the elder President Bush had looked to General Norman Schwarzkopf.

Goal orientation means that a man's spiritual heart will likely zero in on reaching the goal of growth in Christ. Take, for example, Philippians 3:12, where Paul says he presses on to achieve everything for which Christ called him. A woman reads the apostle's words from one perspective and the man another. She likely relates better to the process of growth, and he is more motivated by achieving the result.

Men tend to see spiritual growth as a series of steps to be mastered: read the book, attend the seminar, complete the Bible study. Women gain much from these steps also, but they are more focused on processing input than checking off a list of spiritual accomplishments.

Men relate to God more as a mighty warrior than a tender shepherd. Put another way, we men are more tuned in to God's *transcendence*, viewing Him as exalted and superior, a leader to be followed, whereas women are more attuned to God's *immanence*, the attribute or quality of nearness. God is both, of course: above us as unquestioned superior and beside us as caring shepherd and friend. Men and women just relate to Him differently based on their spiritual wiring.

It's easier for men to relate to God as a warrior king leading the troops into battle. Soldiers don't expect to get up close and personal with their commanding officers, and men in general have a similar awe and respect for God as a superior. It is easier for women to view God as approachable and involved with them. God's immanence is shown in Christ's incarnation. Mary's son, the angel tells Joseph, will be called *Immanuel*, "God with us" (see Matthew 1:23). Immanence pictures softness, a warm bosom, a welcoming lap.

Women perceive God in this way because their spiritual hearts are created to minister immanence in their relationships. This is why wives and mothers are the primary nurturers in their homes and why women in general are more nurturing than men in their friendships. Men see God more as a leader because of our bent to take leadership where we live and work.

Both qualities are needed in relationships, especially marriage. Immanence without transcendence deteriorates to emotional anarchy. Transcendence without immanence becomes cruel tyranny. The two attributes are blended perfectly in the Godhead. Since humans are created in the image of God, immanence and transcendence are wired into us. However, it takes the man and the woman to get the balance. This is one of the reasons God designed marriage to be between a male and a female, not between two men or two women.

God made a man a man and a woman a woman so they could become one flesh. There are varying ideas about when the state of "one flesh" is reached. Some say it happens at the marriage altar, and others say it happens in sexual union. Both of these are true. The biblically based marriage ceremony consecrates a male and female as united in the eyes of God. Paul says sexual union makes people one flesh (see 1 Corinthians 6:16). The realized, manifest, experienced state of "one-fleshness" occurs as the hearts of a man and a woman—over a lifetime—are formed to one another.

Everyone—and that includes us men—needs the nurturing care of a tender shepherd, a caring God who is present with us in our pain and struggle. But we also need the security and guidance of a mighty warrior. In the respective hearts of men and women, God has provided both.

Exercise Your Manly Heart's Uniqueness

Here are four keys for maximizing the unique qualities of a man's spiritual heart.

Exercise Heroic Faith

Noah was a man of heroic faith. God said, "Noah, there's going to be a flood, so build a big boat for your family and a whole menagerie of creatures." Noah immediately got with the program and did as God commanded (see Genesis 6:22). He moved ahead faithfully, even though he had never seen a flood before and no one outside his family was going in God's direction. That's what marked his heroic faith: he believed God when warned about things he'd never seen, and he acted on God's direction though it seemed foolish.

Exercising heroic faith requires that you commit yourself to live as a godly man day by day in an ungodly world—no matter what. Think of this commitment as your sworn allegiance to follow the orders of your Commanding Officer at all costs. You will encounter challenges, temptations, and derision in your daily world, but heroic faith is unwavering in its devotion to God. Follow through on that commitment by obeying God's marching orders even when they seem to make no sense. Building a cargo ship in a landlocked region made Noah look like a nut case in the eyes of his neighbors. But that's what God told him to do, so Noah did it without question.

Maybe you think that Noah had an advantage over you in the faith department. He heard God's voice telling him precisely what to do. It's a lot easier to obey God heroically when you have audible commands. However, you have words from God that are just as clear. Exercise your faith by following the Commander's written orders in the Bible and His inner promptings to your heart. Commit yourself to obedience in all things, and you will know what to do in the small things.

Implement God Dependence

You may not feel an urgent need to attend two to three Bible study groups every week to keep your faith alive and growing. You may get along just fine without male accountability partners with whom you share your deepest struggles and questions. You may feel fine about the fact that you are not in daily conversations with other Christian guys about what you're studying in the Bible. And if you're unable to make it to the church's next men's retreat or the regional Christian men's rally at the arena, you know your faith will survive. These are all excellent ways to strengthen your spiritual heart, and they're worth getting involved in. But like most men, you probably don't depend on experiences like these as much as Christian women tend to.

However, your less-dependent nature doesn't mean you can "lone ranger" your way through life. Just like a woman, you were created to be dependent on God for spiritual life and health. A rogue soldier who does what he thinks is best instead of following orders is of little worth to his commander and the soldiers he serves with—and he's liable to get shot or court-martialed. In the same way, don't think you can keep your spiritual heart healthy without leaning hard on God.

How do you exercise God dependence? Here are three strategies I suggest.

Study. The more you learn about God and grow in relationship with Him, the more confident you will be at depending on Him. And knowing God well doesn't happen apart from the Bible, which is God's instrument for "training us to live God's way" (2 Timothy 3:16 MSG). Read the Bible. Study the Bible. Listen to the Bible on CD as you drive in the car. Read and study books that explain the Bible and help you to know God better. Saturate yourself with what God says, and you equip yourself to follow where God leads.

Relate. Agreed: men don't depend on relationships as much as women do. But we're not supposed to be spiritual hermits either. You need other people—men and women—to encourage your dependence on God. The Bible says, "Let's see how inventive we can be in encouraging love and helping out, not avoiding worshiping together as some do but spurring each other on" (Hebrews 10:24–25 MSG). So get involved with Bible studies, sharing groups and retreats, accountability partners, and so on as you have opportunity. Other people can encourage your dependence on God, and you can encourage theirs.

Lead. Most men I know are not content to remain in entry-level positions. We aspire to succeed, advance, take on more responsibility, and lead others. The same is true in our spiritual wiring. You aren't meant to be a buck private Christian all your life. God calls you to move up the ranks under His command and assume greater responsibility for the development and deployment of others. You'll never experience the fullness of God's leading in your life until you lean on Him to help you lead others, beginning in your home.

Develop Goal-Orientation

I heard about a pastor who sits down with his wife and his children—all nine of them—every New Year to write goals for the coming year. The smaller children are encouraged to set goals for such things as making their beds each morning and memorizing a new Bible verse each week. The older children who are in sports set lofty performance goals. And Dad and Mom talk about their own personal goals, which include how many people they intend to invite to church and hope to lead to Christ during the year. At the end of the year, the family meets again to review their goals, celebrate their accomplishments, and then set even higher standards for the next year.

This pastor leads his church the same way. He sits down with church leaders each year to help them establish realistic, measurable goals for their ministries. During the Easter and Christmas seasons, he challenges church members to write down names of unchurched friends and neighbors they will invite to the special services. Being a goal-driven reader of the Bible himself, the pastor now has his congregation following a plan to read through the Bible each year. Under his leadership, the church has grown in membership from twenty-five to nearly three thousand.

I don't know many men who are as disciplined and purposeful as this pastor. But he's a great example of the importance of utilizing a man's purpose-driven nature to develop a strong spiritual heart. You may have a great deal of experience with setting and accomplishing goals in your business, your finances, your household projects, and even your hobbies. But have you exercised your goal-orientation to enrich your relationship with God?

Here are several possible areas where you might find it profitable to set and pursue goals. I suggest that you select at least one area in which you want to develop greater proficiency and go for it. Raising the bar in this way will help you exercise greater dependence on God.

- Connect daily with God through Bible reading and prayer (frequency, time allotted, time and place, and so on).

- Read through the entire Bible in one to two years.

- Read books that will enhance your study of the Bible and knowledge of God.

- Participate in a Bible study group, prayer group, or accountability group.

- Contact others to invite to church or to a Bible study.

- Initiate relationships with nonbelievers for the purpose of living out and sharing your faith.

- Organize a Bible study or prayer group where you work.

- Take a position of leadership in your church, such as assisting in a Sunday school class or serving on a committee.

Embrace the Nearness of God

You've got a free evening, so you're at the video store picking up a movie to take home. If you're like a lot of guys, you head for the action-adventure section. There's nothing like an exciting "guy flick" that promises guns, bombs, careening cars, blood-and-guts army battles, slimy aliens, or a handful of good guys vanquishing an army of bad guys. After all, gunfire and explosions are why you bought the best home-theater sound system you could afford, right?

Why do we like these kinds of stories? Because men are fighters created in the image of our Warrior King. We like stories of toughness and transcendence because we serve a fearless King. In his book *Wild at Heart,* John Eldredge reminds us, "Aggression is part of the masculine *design*; we are hardwired for it. If we believe that man is made in the image of God, then we would do well to remember that 'the Lord is a warrior; the Lord is his name.'"[2]

But what if you are renting a movie that you and your wife or girlfriend can watch together? Will you still shop in the same section? Probably not. Most women prefer stories involving immanence—relationships, caring, closeness, love—because that's how God shaped their spiritual hearts.

You know that transcendence and immanence are not exclusively male and female traits, don't you? Admit it: you've felt a lump of emotion in your throat while watching a tender scene of bonding or devotion. Father and son resolve a bitter feud and tearfully embrace. A man gives his life to rescue the woman he loves. These images strike a chord in men as well as women—though maybe not as deeply—because we men were created to relate as well as to conquer and to lead.

As a man, you have great capacity for immanence. Embrace God in His nearness, tenderness, and affection. The commander-in-chief of the heavenly armies is also your loving Father who bounces you on His knee and delights to give you presents. Christ your Master is also Jesus your brother and friend.

We can learn something from our women about experiencing the immanence of God. It's okay to weep when overwhelmed by the realization of God's love for you. It's not effeminate to maintain an intimate conversation with God throughout the day as if He is right there with you—because He is! And there's nothing wrong with displaying Christ's immanent love for other guys with a manly embrace. Your spiritual heart will grow strong as you balance your inherent attraction to God's transcendence with your less-apparent but genuine capacity for His immanence.

Every really good guy movie has villains—persons or creatures we love to hate. You will also encounter villains on your journey to Total Heart Health. Unlike the bad guys on the screen, these enemies are real and must be dealt with. In part 2, Mike, Rick, and I will bring into the light the enemies of your spiritual heart and physical heart and show you how to blow them away.

Keys to Total Heart Health

Chapter 3: The Unique Nature
of a Man's Spiritual Heart

- God designed men and women to be distinct. One of the ways to keep your spiritual heart healthy is to affirm the man God made you to be and relate to Him just as you are.

- Generally, men are physically larger than women because God created us to protect and serve those not as strong, whether men, women, or children.

- Men are emotionally different from women, equating maturity with independence, while women see it as interdependence.

- Men generally are spiritually different from women in that men seek heroic faith, are less dependent, are more goal-driven, and relate to God more as mighty warrior than tender shepherd.

- Four keys to exercising the uniqueness of a man's heart:

  1. *Exercise heroic faith.* Commit yourself to live as a godly man day by day in an ungodly world, no matter what.

  2. *Implement dependence on God.* Study the Bible; relate to other people by getting involved in Bible studies, small groups, and accountability partnerships; and lead others to know and grow in God.

  3. *Develop goal-orientation.* Select areas in your life in which you want to develop greater proficiency, because raising the bar will help you exercise greater dependence on God.

  4. *Embrace the nearness of God.* Also focus on becoming more relational, caring, loving, and intimate, especially with those nearest and dearest to you.

Part 2

The Crippling Enemies
of a Man's Heart

4
Caught in the Cross Hairs

Your heart was built to last, but a lethal predator is out to change that.

Dr. Ed Young

Someone very powerful and devious is dead set against the healthy heart God has designed you to have. This enemy's target is the heart of every man and woman, and he is particularly interested in ruining the lives of people who want to take God seriously. This enemy, of course, is the enemy of our souls and God's archenemy: Satan himself.

Now, please don't think I'm going off the deep end spiritually, wondering if I see a demon under every rock and behind every door just waiting to tackle you and drag you away against your will. Nor am I saying that the devil is personally responsible for everything wrong and hurtful in our lives. We are imperfect people living in an imperfect world, and bad things happen. But if you dismiss the sobering biblical reality that Satan is out to keep you from God's goodness in your life, you will be especially vulnerable to his destructive schemes, and your total heart will be at great risk.

The conflict between what God has for us and what Satan intends to do about it is no more clearly and concisely stated than in John 10:10. Jesus said, "A thief is only there to steal and kill and destroy. I came so they can have real and eternal life, more and better life than they ever dreamed of" (MSG). We really like the second half of that verse, don't we, especially the idea of a better, more abundant life? It is often quoted all by itself, as if the first half of the verse didn't exist. But watch out: there really is a thief plotting against you.

The abundant life that Jesus describes here is even better than most of us have imagined. Two Greek words in the New Testament are translated "life."

One of them is *bios*, referring to biological life, natural life. We can't live in a world of time, space, and matter without biological structure—a living, breathing body; oxygen; food; and natural laws in place to make it all work. The other word translated "life," which occurs in John 10:10, is *zoe*, meaning spiritual life, life on God's plane. When you see the phrase "everlasting life" or "eternal life" in the New Testament, the word translated "life" is *zoe*. It's the same word Jesus used when announcing, "I am the way, and the truth, and the life" (John 14:6); "I am the bread of life" (John 6:35); and "I am the resurrection and the life" (John 11:25).

We received *bios* when we were conceived and born into this world. Jesus came to bring us *zoe*, which not only infinitely enhances the quality of our biological existence but supersedes it both now and throughout eternity. And in John 10:10, Jesus qualified the life He gives with the word *abundantly*, meaning "over and above; more than necessary." It's the same picture Paul used to describe our God, who can do anything, "far more than you could ever imagine or guess or request in your wildest dreams!" (Ephesians 3:20 MSG).

Why has God lavished the fullness of His life on us? It's not just for our benefit. It goes far beyond our mere fulfillment and enjoyment. As Rick Warren so pointedly reminds us in *The Purpose Driven Life*, "You were made *by* God and *for* God—and until you understand that, life will never make sense. . . . Life is about letting God use you for *his* purposes."[1] We have God's abundant life *in us* so God's abundant love can flow *through us* to touch the hearts of other people.

Killer on the Loose

God's exciting purposes for your life are precisely why Satan is your sworn enemy. He is diametrically opposed to everything God is and does; so if you're in God's camp, you are Satan's target. But he's not out just to wound you; he's aiming to take you out. He wants to neutralize your impact for Christ in the world. He wants to kill your heart.

How does he do it? John 10:10 uses three words: *steal, kill,* and *destroy.* "Steal" in this verse is the Greek word *klepto*, from which we get our English word *kleptomaniac*—an impulsive thief. The word *thief* in this verse comes from the same root. It means to sneak in and take something by stealth. The devil is out to filch every good thing God has given to you. It's the same picture we get in the parable of the soils when Jesus said, "The devil comes and takes away [*klepto*] the word from their heart, so that they will not believe and be saved" (Luke 8:12).

But Satan doesn't burst in to rob you with an Uzi blazing. He's a con artist, a scammer. We are to be wary of his "schemes" (Ephesians 6:11), which are cunning, deceitful, and crafty. He wants to fool with your mind and con you out of the good things God has given you before you know what hit you.

"Kill" has no secret, obscure meaning; it means to put to death, like an animal slaughtered for a sacrifice. In Romans 12:1, Paul urges us to present ourselves to God as living sacrifices. By stark contrast, Satan just wants us dead. He will do everything in his power to snuff out our spiritual life. He can't take away our salvation, but he can do his best to separate us from life-sustaining involvement in God's Word, in prayer, and in fellowship with other Christians.

Satan not only wants to suffocate your spiritual heart, he will do whatever he can to take away your physical heart. Jesus labeled the devil a "murderer" (John 8:44). Satan is out to cause your physical death if he possibly can. Why does Satan want you physically dead? Because it would bring an abrupt end to your loving care for others, and the whole purpose to which God has called you. With you out of the way, he has eliminated a key person God wants to use to touch your family members, your neighbors, your friends, and others in your circle of influence.

How can he get rid of you? Well, he knows you're too smart to fall for the temptation to jump off a bridge, throw yourself in front of a speeding train, or drink a bottle of cyanide—although he may introduce such drastic thoughts when you're discouraged or depressed. Remember: he's a con artist. He wants to trick you into doing his bidding, to cause you to think it's not too bad. So he might just suggest more acceptable behaviors that could eventually gain him the same result, behaviors that will negatively affect your health.

We cannot presume that we are physically invincible just because we are Christians. If we mistreat our bodies through poor diet and lack of proper exercise, we will pay the price for it. Such irresponsible behavior may not kill us outright, but it may open the door to problems like heart disease or cancer, which will usher death into the picture ahead of schedule. And in the mean-time, the enemy can disrupt and disable our lives through sickness, which also thwarts God's purposes for us in the world.

Jesus also said the devil comes to "destroy," which means to render useless. He is always intent on destroying our abundance and vitality, leaving our lives a barren desert and useless ruin. You've probably heard the familiar saying, "God don't make no junk." Well, the devil specializes in filling our lives with junk. He can't make you into junk, but he can tempt you to believe you are no good to God or anybody. In this way he will try to destroy you physically, emotionally, spiritually, intellectually, and relationally.

How does the enemy go about his business of stealing, killing, and destroy-ing? The New Testament reveals many of Satan's strategies designed to trick you into thoughts and deeds that will ruin a man's heart and render him use-less to God and others. Here are some of them:

- He tempts us to do the opposite of what God wants (see 1 Thessalonians 3:5).

- He works to oppress us, meaning to exercise harsh control (see Acts 10:38).

- He seeks to devour us, swallow us (see 1 Peter 5:8).

- He tries to bind us, tie us up, and keep us from moving forward (see Luke 13:16).

- He disguises himself to look attractive and appealing (see 2 Corinthians 11:14).

- He hinders us, meaning to block our course or cut us off (see 1 Thessalonians 2:18).

- He lies to us, because he is a liar by nature (see John 8:44).

Tools of the Enemy's Trade

As mentioned earlier, I don't believe the Bible teaches that the devil or even one of his demons is personally responsible for every lapse you suffer in the care of your heart. He is certainly at the root of all the evil we suffer, but he has some "accomplices" who do much of his dirty work for him.

Lust

One of the big ones for men is lust, which is the longing or desire to please our flesh and get what we want as opposed to pleasing and obeying God. James wrote, "The temptation to give in to evil comes from us and only us. We have no one to blame but the leering, seducing flare-up of our own lust. Lust gets pregnant, and has a baby: sin! Sin grows up to adulthood, and becomes a real killer" (James 1:14–15 MSG).

Lust arises from the old habits, feelings, and thoughts we operated by before God made our hearts come alive through Christ. For men, lust isn't just about illicit sex and sexual fantasies. It's also about things like power, control, and possessions. These old selfish patterns keep demanding their way. When we obey these lustful longings, we sin; and these sins move us in the direction of disease and death to the total heart.

The Godless World System

Another one of Satan's accomplices in attacking our hearts is the godless world system in which we live. The apostle John wrote, "Practically everything that goes on in the world—wanting your own way, wanting everything for yourself, wanting to appear important—has nothing to do with the Father. It just isolates you from him" (1 John 2:16 MSG). Much of our lust is triggered by what we see, hear, and experience in a world that puts selfish pleasures above God.

For example, as you well know, the world bombards us with images of immorality through the media: movies, television, the Internet, novels, and magazines. Faithful monogamy and sex reserved only for marriage are portrayed as archaic and odd, while adultery, illicit affairs, and casual sex between consenting adults and teens are glorified as normal and right. Being exposed to so many episodes of bedroom roulette in the media—and in the public lives of celebrities—we may wonder if God's view of moral purity is outdated. No wonder so many Christians today, including some of our respected leaders, are caving in to sexual temptation.

The world's misguided idea of right and wrong comes at us from every direction, tempting us to compromise biblical standards for honesty, truth, righteousness, humility, and service to others. Falling prey to this accomplice of the enemy will weaken your heart instead of strengthen it.

And look at how the world attacks your physical heart. So many advertisements on TV make unhealthy foods look desirable and convenient. Why eat healthy food at home when it's so easy and inexpensive to drive through a fast-food place—any time of the day or night? Why order a regular-sized portion of French fries when the large and extra-large portions cost only a little more? The food industry is out to make money, so their ads will promote quantity, convenience, and flavor over sensible portions and healthy ingredients.

If we allow the world to sway us with its message about food, the fallout will diminish the health of our physical hearts. Drs. Duncan and Leachman will talk more specifically about these dangers in the chapters ahead.

Stand Guard Over Your Heart

Solomon had keen insight into the assault of the world, the flesh, and the devil on the total heart, leaving us the important directive "Guard your heart" (Proverbs 4:23 NLT). His wise warning must be heeded. The abundant life Christ has for us is under constant attack. If you don't fight for the health of your total heart, who will?

How can you stand up to the enemy's malicious opposition? The Word of God provides some straightforward, hope-filled answers.

Keep Alert to the Enemy's Attempts to Attack You

"Keep a cool head. Stay alert. The Devil is poised to pounce, and would like nothing better than to catch you napping. Keep your guard up" (1 Peter 5:8–9 MSG). Don't minimize Satan's cunning, which is more dangerous than a stalking, hungry lion out for a kill.

Send the Enemy Packing

Peter says about the roaring lion, "Resist him, firm in your faith" (1 Peter 5:9). James says, "So let God work his will in you. Yell a loud *no* to the Devil and watch him scamper" (James 4:7 MSG). For all his craft and cunning,

Satan is outranked by a believer who is submitted to the authority of Christ, and he must obey your orders. Whenever this conniving thief and liar or one of his accomplices threatens your heart, you have every right in Christ to tell him to get lost.

In God's unsearchable wisdom, He has called you and equipped you for this battle for your heart. *You* must be alert. *You* must resist the enemy of your heart in Christ's power and authority. As you do, you are being effectively proactive in improving your Total Heart Health.

Before we look closer at some other ways your spiritual heart is under attack, Drs. Duncan and Leachman will alert us to some serious threats to your physical heart. Guarding your physical heart is an important element in our 90-Day Challenge and Total Heart Health lifestyle.

Keys to Total Heart Health
Chapter 4: Caught in the Cross Hairs

- The devil's target is the heart of every man and woman, and he is particularly interested in ruining the lives of people who take God seriously.

- If you dismiss the biblical reality that Satan is out to keep you from God's goodness in your life, you will be especially vulnerable to his destructive schemes, and your total heart is at great risk.

- We have God's abundant life *in us* so God's abundant love can flow *through us* to touch the hearts of other people.

- Satan not only wants to suffocate your spiritual heart, he will do whatever he can to take away your physical heart, because that would bring an abrupt end to the purpose to which God has called you.

- If we mistreat our physical bodies, the enemy can disrupt and disable our lives through sickness, which also thwarts God's purposes for us in the world.

- The devil and his demons aren't responsible for every lapse we suffer in caring for our hearts, but he is at the root of all the evil we suffer.

- Satan has several accomplices in carrying out his dirty work, including lust and the godless world system.

- The Bible shows how you can guard your heart: stay alert to the enemy's attempts to attack you, and send the enemy packing.

- As you resist the enemies of your heart through Christ's power, you are being effectively proactive in improving your Total Heart Health.

5

The Hidden Killer

Heads up: heart disease doesn't just happen
to the other guy.

Dr. Michael Duncan and Dr. Richard Leachman

Bernie attributes his wife, Ruth, with saving his life. He was jogging on the treadmill in the basement when he felt a sudden dull pain in his chest. He gasped and moaned and gripped his chest as he cut the power on the machine. Ruth, who was sorting laundry nearby, heard him. "What's wrong?"

"Nothing," Bernie said, grimacing and doubled over. "It's just a gas pain under my heart." Then he rubbed his left arm and hissed in pain.

"It might be worse than you think," Ruth said, alarmed. "Chest pain and left arm pain: those are symptoms of a heart attack. I'm taking you to the emergency room."

Bernie resisted, but Ruth would not be denied. Within thirty minutes, they were at the hospital. At six the next morning, Bernie was wheeled into the operating room for quadruple-bypass surgery. The surgeon explained that if Bernie had not come in when he did, he could have dropped dead during a subsequent treadmill exercise.

The Number One Heart Killer

Cardiovascular disease (CVD) is the number one health threat to men and the leading cause of death in the United States and the Western world. *Cardiovascular disease* is a generic term inclusive of a number of maladies afflicting the heart and coronary arteries, such as atherosclerosis (plaque buildup in the arteries), stroke, and heart attack. The American Heart Association reports that CVD claims the lives of 440,000 men a year, more than the next four causes of death combined: cancer, accidents, chronic lower respiratory diseases, and diabetes.[1]

There are notable differences between men and women when it comes to cardiovascular disease. This information will be especially important if, in addition to your own heart health, you are concerned about the heart health of a wife, fiancée, mother, sister, or other female loved ones.

Overall, the prevalence of heart disease in men is slightly higher than in women, but more women than men die from CVD, about a half million per year.[2] Heart disease increases proportionately in women in every age group up into the sixties. In the sixty-five to seventy-four age group, women finally catch up to men, with an equal prevalence of CVD in both sexes. Above age seventy-five, women surpass men in the prevalence of heart disease.[3] Statistically, as a woman gets older, she is at greater risk of some form of cardiovascular disease than a man.[4]

What is even more disconcerting is that the incidence of CVD-related deaths is *decreasing* in men but *increasing* in women. Here's what the studies reveal:

- During the last twenty-five years, the number of deaths attributed to cardiovascular disease in men has declined from 510,000 to less than 440,000. During the same time frame, female deaths from CVD have increased from 490,000 to nearly 510,000.[5]

- Women are more likely than men to die after a cardiac event. Thirty-eight percent of women who have had a heart attack die within one year; only 25 percent of men die within one year.[6]

- Sixty-three percent of women who die suddenly have no prior diagnosis of cardiovascular disease, compared to 50 percent of men.

- Within six years after a recognized heart attack, 35 percent of women will have another heart attack, 14 percent will develop angina (chest pain), 11 percent will have a stroke, 6 percent will die, and 46 percent will develop heart failure.[7]

What is the reason for such a difference between men and women? It may be that the message is more forcefully delivered to men to reduce heart-disease risks (i.e., to quit smoking, manage cholesterol, control hypertension and diabetes), while women hear more about the risks of breast cancer. Since heart disease is less of a concern early in life, women typically do not go to the doctor until they have already developed unstable angina or are having a heart attack. When they are diagnosed with heart disease, they generally have more advanced disease. Intervention is both riskier and more difficult, and they are more likely than men to die from heart disease.

Since the risk of cardiovascular disease is greater in men before the senior years, we encourage you to see your doctor regularly for checkups. At the same time, encourage the women in your life to monitor heart health throughout all stages of life, but especially from the onset of menopause.

Another reason for the greater number of CVD-related deaths in women relates to the different symptoms experienced by the sexes. Signs and symptoms of heart problems are more specific in men, leading to quicker intervention, whereas a woman's symptoms can be easily overlooked. Women and their doctors may be "faked out" by atypical symptoms of heart disease, which contributes to a delay in diagnosis.

The following chart compares the gender differences related to heart-attack symptoms.[8]

Gender Differences in Symptoms of Heart Attack

Men's Symptoms	Women's Symptoms
Chest pain or pressure	Pain in chest, upper back, jaw, or neck
Pain while resting	Shortness of breath
Pain down left arm and shoulder	Flulike symptoms: nausea, vomiting, cold sweats
Weakness	Fatigue or weakness
	Feeling of anxiety, loss of appetite, malaise

This study raises a red flag for men to pay attention to the signs and symptoms experienced by female loved ones that could indicate heart problems. If you notice the sudden onset of unusual symptoms or a change of symptoms in the women in your life, you should encourage them to see a doctor.

Major Health Risks to a Man's Heart

Another difference between men and women when it comes to heart disease relates to the outcome after heart surgery. More than 500,000 coronary-artery-bypass graft (CABG) procedures—in layperson's terms, bypass surgeries—are performed in this country every year. About 350,000 of them are performed on men. Yet, as a rule, men fare far better than women with respect to the seriousness of CVD (morbidity) and death rate (mortality).[9]

There are several reasons for this, some of which are fairly obvious.

First, compared to women, men generally are taller, weigh more, and have a larger body surface area. This means men generally have larger coronary arteries, which do not clog as readily as the smaller arteries in women. And the smaller size of women's coronary arteries presents a greater technical challenge for performing angioplasty or bypass surgery.

Second, because estrogen is thought to provide a protective effect against cardiovascular disease, women are rarely affected by CVD before menopause. As such, most women are older and in worse overall physical condition when they do require treatment.

Finally, women are also more likely to have the complications of "co-morbid" conditions, including diabetes, high blood pressure, congestive heart failure, obesity, and cerebral or peripheral vascular disease (disease that restricts circulation to the brain or extremities).[10]

In addition to gender-related risks, there are a number of other factors that can lead to cardiovascular disease in both men and women. These are called risk factors. Risk factors are divided into two categories: major and contributing. The major risk factors are those that have been proved to increase the risk of heart disease. Contributing factors are those that doctors think can lead to an increased risk, but the exact role they play may not be defined.

Only one of the major risk factors is not preventable: family history. If your parents or grandparents were plagued by cardiovascular disease, you are at a higher risk of CVD than the man whose forebears had a clean bill of heart health. However, four risk factors for heart disease are largely preventable through diet, exercise, and lifestyle. Here are six of the major risk factors with a brief explanation of each.

Smoking

Cigarette smoking has been medically determined to be a major risk factor for coronary artery disease (CAD). Smoking is generally linked to a more severe form of atherosclerosis than that which occurs from poor diet. Smokers have at least a 200 percent greater risk of developing coronary heart disease than non-smokers. Smoking causes a variety of adverse physical responses that result in accelerated production of plaque in the coronary arteries (hardening of the arteries). Increased plaque also heightens the risk of blood clots, which cause heart attacks. Smoking has also been shown to increase LDL (bad cholesterol) and decrease HDL (good cholesterol). We can't say this too strongly: *smoking will kill your heart; don't smoke!*

High Cholesterol

Hyperlipidemia refers to a high level of fats circulating in the bloodstream. In some patients, these levels are genetically determined. Cholesterol is one of the groups that make up the fatty or lipid compounds in the bloodstream. Cholesterol is produced by the liver. The amount of cholesterol circulating in the blood is also affected by weight, diet, and exercise.

Most cholesterol is transported to the body's cells in small particles called low-density lipoprotein (LDL). High levels of LDL are associated with increased risk for heart disease, earning it the designation of "bad cholesterol." When LDL levels are high, resulting from a diet of high-cholesterol foods, they deposit on the walls of the arteries as plaque. Over a period of time, the plaque can cause obstruction or occlusion of an artery, triggering a heart attack.

Diabetes

Diabetes, categorized as Type I and Type II, is a disease in which the body cannot process sugar—glucose—in the normal fashion. Type I diabetes, also called insulin-dependent, child-onset, or juvenile diabetes, results when the pancreas no longer produces insulin, which is necessary for the body to process glucose from the blood to the cells. Type I diabetes patients must receive regular insulin injections to live.

Type II diabetes, also called non-insulin-dependent or adult-onset diabetes, results when the pancreas does not produce enough insulin or the cells in the body ignore the insulin. When glucose builds up in the bloodstream instead of going into the cells, your cells may become starved for energy. Over time, high blood-glucose levels can cause kidney disease, blindness, atherosclerosis, and heart disease.

An alarming 6 percent of the U.S. population (15.7 million people) have diabetes, and this reality cannot be dismissed as wholly congenital. Cultural environment—such as the bad information about food and consumption we get on TV—and personal behavior—such as overeating and too much fat in the diet—are primarily at fault in the soaring numbers of adult diabetic patients.

Persons with diabetes also tend to have other traits that make them more at risk for developing heart problems. These include obesity, a sedentary lifestyle, high blood pressure, and high cholesterol.

Hypertension

Hypertension is the medical term for high blood pressure. The American Heart Association estimates that more than fifty million Americans suffer from hypertension, including one of every four adults. Hypertension is the leading cause of stroke and a major risk factor for heart attack and kidney failure. There are no typical symptoms for hypertension, so without periodic blood pressure screenings, you may be unaware of its presence.

Obesity

Obesity is defined as a body mass index greater than 30. Body mass index will be more fully explained in chapter 7. Obesity has been directly associated with increased risk of heart disease, including hypertension, hyperlipidemia, diabetes, and vascular disease. Weight reduction for obese persons significantly decreases these problems and therefore lowers the risk of developing coronary heart disease.

Family History

Some forms of heart disease are inherited from family members, and some may lie undetected until it is too late. *If you have a family history of heart disease, particularly in your parents, it is important that you see your doctor regularly to monitor your physical condition.* Even without a known background of heart problems in your family, you are wise to take advantage of all preventive measures to keep your heart healthy, including periodic physical exams, a healthy diet, and regular exercise.

Coronary artery disease is your physical heart's number one enemy. In this book, we will give you solid medical counsel on how you can guard your physical heart and maximize your opportunity to live a long, quality life by taking good care of your heart. We join Dr. Ed Young in urging you to make a commitment to a Total Heart Health lifestyle, both for yourself and for your family.

Your spiritual heart is also under assault and in need of proactive care. In the next chapter, Dr. Young will talk about spiritual heart disease, how to avoid it, and how to find healing from it.

Keys to Total Heart Health

Chapter 5: The Hidden Killer

- Cardiovascular disease (CVD) is the number one health threat to men and the leading cause of death in the United States and the Western world.

- Risk factors are divided into two categories, major and contributing. Major factors are those proven to increase the risk of heart disease, and contributing factors are those doctors think can lead to higher risk.

- Major risk factors for CVD:

    1. *Family history.* If your parents or grandparents had CVD, you are at a higher risk. Family history is the only risk factor that is not preventable.

    2. *Smoking.* Smokers have a 200 percent greater risk of developing coronary heart disease than nonsmokers.

    3. *High cholesterol.* The amount of cholesterol circulating in the blood is affected by weight, diet, and exercise.

    4. *Diabetes.* Cultural environment and personal behavior are primarily at fault in the soaring number of adult diabetes patients.

    5. *Obesity.* Weight reduction for obese persons significantly decreases the risk of developing CVD.

- It is vital to make a commitment to a Total Heart Health lifestyle, both for yourself and for your family.

6

Ominous Signs
of Spiritual Heart Disease

Okay, so you can ace a stress test.
But is your heart for God just as strong?

Dr. Ed Young

As a young man in his thirties, Jeb Stuart Magruder was tapped for one of the most powerful political jobs in America. He was appointed deputy director of Richard Nixon's 1972 reelection campaign against challenger Senator Edmund Muskie. Ten years earlier, Magruder had gained a reputation as a skilled political operative by managing Donald Rumsfeld's campaign for a seat in the House of Representatives. During the next several years, Magruder continued his rise and was eventually named special assistant to the president. If he succeeded in getting Nixon reelected, he could practically name his job in the White House. The future couldn't have looked brighter for this tall, lean, intelligent young man.

The campaign was a resounding success, producing one of the most lopsided victories in history. Nixon thundered back into office, winning forty-nine of fifty states, plus the District of Columbia. Magruder was then tapped to direct Nixon's 1973 inauguration. In the eyes of many in Washington, Jeb Magruder had arrived at the top on the fast track. No one knew at that time it was a fast track to a dead end.

Early in Nixon's second term, there were hints about the secrets that were plaguing Jeb Magruder. His friends in the White House saw the gray in his hair, the sag in his posture, and the dark weariness and worry in his eyes. Most assumed he was simply wearing the pressures of the campaign. But Magruder knew the truth: a team under the auspices of his political organization had broken into the headquarters of the National Democratic Party in Washington's Watergate complex in an attempt to bug the phone of its director. The burglars had been caught, and Magruder knew the threads would eventually be followed back to him and his associates.

Months later, Magruder became the second official in the Nixon administration to plead guilty to involvement in the Watergate scandal. When asked how he had allowed himself to become party to such a crime, Magruder hung his head and said, "I don't know. I guess I just lost my moral compass."

Jeb Stuart Magruder, the sharp young man with so much promise, was sentenced to a federal prison near Allenwood, Pennsylvania, where he spent seven months. His heart was crushed to the point that some of his friends and associates wondered if he would ever recover.

Thankfully, Magruder's story doesn't end there. His heart, which had been pulverized in the heartless machinery of Washington, began to heal in prison. Magruder became a follower of Christ. After prison, he attended Princeton Theological Seminary, earning a master's of divinity degree in 1981. As a minister, Reverend Magruder used the testimony of his own failure and healing to help others with a painful past find healing.

Just as the ravages of cardiovascular disease can cripple and kill the physical heart, so a sense of failure, hopelessness, and resignation can imprison the spiritual heart. The enemy of your heart would like nothing better than to weaken you to the point of ineffectiveness in your service to Christ, your family, your church, and the needy world around you. And being a sly, conniving thief, he will work in the shadows to exploit any weakness or injury of the soul in order to infect your heart with disabling disease. When you are bowed down under fear and resignation, you will feel worthless to yourself, to God, and to others. And that's just where the devil wants you.

What are the signs of spiritual disease encroaching on a man's heart? I want to share with you five risk factors that promote a sagging spiritual heart and how Jesus Christ can help you confront and neutralize their threat and live with renewed hope and expectation.

Spiritual Baggage

As Drs. Duncan and Leachman have explained, your family health history is one of the primary determinants for your physical health. If your parents were victims of some form of cardiovascular disease, you are at greater risk of encountering similar problems and must be doubly careful to guard your heart. And for those unfortunate enough to have inherited a propensity for heart disease, there is not much that can be done about changing it.

When it comes to the spiritual heart, your family can also deal you a potentially losing hand. For example, you may have grown up in a home where you were robbed of parental acceptance and approval. Your heart may bear the scars of any number of difficulties in your growing-up family: physical, sexual, or emotional abuse; alcoholism; divorce; poverty; occult activity; abandonment; or other hurtful treatment. Even as a Christian, you may feel shackled to your dysfunctional past because emotional and spiritual heredity has such a tight grip on your heart.

Unlike physical heredity, you *can* do something about your spiritual heredity. The key to overcoming a painful family history is to focus on who you *are* instead of who you *were*. The man dominated by the old life lives in "I was-ness." But God is always "I Am," and those restored to the Father are empowered to live in "I Am-ness."

No matter how your spirit was stifled or stunted in the past, if you are a child of God, you have been adopted into a new family spiritually. God is your Father now, and He accepts you unconditionally because of what Jesus Christ did on the cross. Paul wrote, "Those who become Christians become new persons. They are not the same anymore, for the old life is gone. A new life has begun!" (2 Corinthians 5:17 NLT). Your life is in the hands of One who will never abuse you, ignore you, abandon you, or fail you. Whenever you are haunted by hurts from the past, begin to praise God for who you are in Christ. And if a painful upbringing has stunted your progress in following God, we encourage you to seek wise counsel to help you work through your difficult issues.

Spiritual Deafness

A young man went off to college. "Promise me one thing," his mother said before he left home. "Promise me you will be in church every Sunday." This loving son promised he would do what she asked.

At college, one of the boy's new friends invited him to his family's ranch for a weekend. On Saturday evening, the host said, "Tomorrow we're going to ride horses to the lake and fish all day." On Sunday morning, as they rode out, our young friend heard the peal of a church bell in the distance, but he nudged his horse onward. Again the bell sounded, but this time fainter. The young man kept riding. The third time, the bell was barely audible. Suddenly, this college freshman turned his horse around and started riding back.

"Where are you going?" his host asked.

The young man replied, "I have to turn back while I can still hear the bell."

God never ceases to call to us and offer us His strength for our hearts. But life's activities, demands, and distractions can draw us out of the range of the bell, and we begin to lose our heart, our passion for God and life. Don't neglect the bell while you can still hear it!

In Proverbs 1:24–25, wisdom—which is equated with the fear of the Lord—speaks: "I called and you refused, I stretched out my hand and no one paid attention; and you neglected all my counsel and did not want my reproof." The Hebrew word translated "counsel" means plans or strategies. God will help you overcome spiritual heart disease if you heed His strategies. But if you neglect Him and wander far from His call, the sad payoff will be "calamity," "dread," "distress," and "anguish" (vv. 26–27).

Spiritual Malnutrition

Some men who have been following Christ for a long time still struggle mightily in the battle against temptation. They just don't seem to have the spiritual muscle to consistently say no, so they live with hearts clouded by defeat and shame. Why is this so? Well, when you're physically malnourished, it's usually because you're not eating right or taking needed vitamin supplements. The same is true for spiritual malnutrition. If you're not eating right spiritually, you will lack the heart power to resist temptation and grow strong.

I call this the "Corinthian syndrome." In 1 Corinthians 3, Paul lamented that the church at Corinth could only stomach spiritual milk when he wanted to serve them meat. They were spiritual babies when they should have been more mature. That's the sad diagnosis for a lot of Christian men today. They invest a lot of free time in reading Christian novels and listening to music, recorded sermons, and TV programs that provide a religious "buzz." They are getting a lot to "eat" spiritually, but most of it is "milk." Their approach to Bible study is a mile wide and an inch deep. No wonder they lack the strength to withstand temptation.

We all know the health risks of eating too much fast food—high calories, high fat, low nutritional value. Trying to stay alive on "fast faith" instead of regular, substantial feedings on the Word of God will leave your spiritual heart malnourished, weak, and vulnerable. God asks His people, "Why do you spend money for what is not bread, and your wages for what does not satisfy?" (Isaiah 55:2). He's talking about spiritual food here. The solution to this problem is in the same verse: "Listen carefully to Me, and eat what is good, and delight yourself in abundance."

Jesus said, "I am the bread of life; he who comes to Me will not hunger, and he who believes in Me will never thirst" (John 6:35). It is vital to the health and strength of your spiritual heart that you feed daily on Christ and His Word through purposeful Bible study and prayer. We will talk more about formulating a healthy spiritual diet in chapter 14.

Spiritual Atrophy

Another side of the spiritual anemia many men face is a lack of spiritual exercise. Not only are they not eating enough lean spiritual meat, but they aren't exercising their faith. They attend church, read books, and listen to tapes to get something for themselves. But they aren't doing anything in ministry for others. They are spiritual couch potatoes; they don't "work out" their salvation through deliberate acts of service (see Philippians 2:12). As a result, they have little spiritual muscle for their ongoing warfare against temptation.

Our two heart doctors will be talking about the importance of energy balance for a healthy physical heart. You need a good balance between the energy you take in—food—and the energy you expend—physical activity and exercise. For most of us, our energy is out of balance; we take in too much and expend too little. The result is that more than half of our population is clinically overweight, which leads to all kinds of physical problems.

Energy balance is just as important to spiritual vitality. We need "energy in"—a healthy spiritual diet of consistent Bible study, prayer, and worship—and we need "energy out"—a disciplined approach to serving God and others through activities of helpfulness. Too little spiritual exercise, and you get spiritually flabby. It's important to keep in shape and develop good muscle tone by staying spiritually active. Find ways to use your unique abilities to display God's love and help others in your church and community. We will share much more about spiritual "energy out" in chapter 16.

Spiritual Paralysis

Another debilitating ailment threatening the health of a man's spiritual heart is the fear of failure. Growth and change are part of life. The Christian should always be learning, maturing, and expanding his borders as a servant of Christ. Even the apostle Paul recognized that he had not "arrived" at complete spiritual perfection or maturity; he was a work in progress. He wrote of his ongoing development in Christ, "Forgetting what lies behind and reaching forward to what lies ahead, I press on toward the goal for the prize of the upward call of God in Christ Jesus" (Philippians 3:13–14).

Your heart for God and ministry in His kingdom has limitless growth potential. Indeed, if your spiritual heart isn't in a growth mode, it is in danger of atrophying. But growth isn't easy. In Paul's words, it requires reaching forward and pressing onward. These words picture a race in which the competitors are sprinting, stretching, and straining toward the tape in order to win the gold medal.

The problem is that a lot of Christians never leave the starting line. They are paralyzed by a fear of failure. Or they start into the race and give up because there are too many obstacles or disappointments. They say things like, "I've tried this before and it didn't work," or "I'm going to fall flat on my face and look like a fool," or "I'm just not good enough, so why try?"

If you have ever experienced a setback or a disappointment as a Christian, you know what I mean. Every year you vow to read through the Bible, but you've never made it past the book of Job. You tried to start a Bible study group at work, but nobody came. You want family Bible reading to be meaningful to your kids, but every attempt is a joke to them. A non-Christian at the gym cussed you out when you shared your faith with him, so you aren't ready to try that again. You compare your meager efforts for Christ with the accomplishments of other Christian men you know, and you say, "I'm nothing." Or perhaps a sinful past mocks any attempt at moving forward with Christ.

One of the keys to overcoming your fear of failure and moving forward toward a stronger spiritual heart is to *not* look backward. Paul said, "Forgetting what lies behind . . ." In this race, everybody trips and falls occasionally. Everybody makes a wrong turn. Everybody pulls up lame. Everybody "hits the wall" with fatigue. The idea is not to run without mistakes; the idea is to stay in the race and finish well. Every man who perseveres and finishes gets a gold medal. When you hit an obstacle or experience failure, you just leave it in the past, focus on the finish line, and keep going.

Bobby Richardson, all-star second baseman for the New York Yankees from 1955 to 1966, is a personal friend of mine who has focused on the finish line. When he signed with the Yankees, Bobby was a committed follower of Christ, and his faith only became stronger in the face of fame's pressures and temptations. An outstanding player, Bobby played with some of the greatest in the game: Mickey Mantle, Roger Maris, Yogi Bera, Whitey Ford, Tony Kubek.

Many years ago, when I was a pastor in Columbia, South Carolina, Bobby Richardson was baseball coach at the University of South Carolina. He phoned me one day and invited me to the "Roost," the athletic dorm at the university. Mickey Mantle and Whitey Ford were going to be there. I dropped everything, collected my sons, and headed for the Roost.

It was fascinating to listen as Bobby, Mickey, and Whitey reminisced. They laughed about their road trips. Mickey and Whitey recalled that most of the team caroused and partied during their free time. But Bobby would go to the YMCA in town and play Ping-Pong. Then he would find a local church where he could attend Bible study or a prayer meeting. His teammates used to kid him about his God-fearing, clean-living ways. As a famous ballplayer traveling the country with the Yankees, Bobby Richardson could have done everything his teammates did, but he chose Ping-Pong, prayer meetings, and Bible studies. "Something's wrong with you," his colleagues used to tell him. But Bobby lived out his convictions and shared his faith in Christ with his teammates whenever he could.

When Mickey Mantle died in 1995, I thought back to the day I sat and talked with those baseball greats. Bobby had tried to share his faith with Mickey later in life, but without apparent success. As a hard drinker, Mantle had been in and out of rehab and underwent a liver transplant shortly before he died. Mickey's four sons also struggled with alcohol. Asked if he was a role model, Mickey said he wouldn't want anyone to follow the kind of life he'd lived.

Mickey Mantle and Bobby Richardson both felt the intense pressures of high-profile living. Mickey, by his own admission, was crushed beneath the life he chose. But Bobby Richardson held firm. What was the difference? The health of the spiritual heart. Mickey Mantle trashed his body with alcohol and ignored God's invitation through his Christian teammate. Bobby said no to the momentary pleasures of this life while proactively nurturing his spiritual heart.

If you want to successfully confront and neutralize the risk factors for spiritual heart disease, you need to be a man of hope. Often we think of hope as a wish for something to happen. For example, you enter your name in a sweepstakes for $5,000 worth of power tools or a new pickup, hoping—wishing—you will win the prize. The problem is, there may be millions of guys across the country wishing and hoping for the same thing, and only one person's hopes will be realized.

That's not the kind of hope we're talking about. The New Testament word translated "hope" means to anticipate a desired outcome with expectation. If God has promised it, if God is the power behind it, you don't have to wish for it—because it's going to happen. In Texas-speak, we say, "It's a done deal."

Has God promised you success in the journey to spiritual maturity? Yes. Does He take primary responsibility for the health of your spiritual heart? Absolutely! Paul exclaimed, "I am confident of this very thing, that He who began a good work in you will perfect it until the day of Christ Jesus" (Philippians 1:6). He's the One who got you out of the starting blocks and into the race in the first place in response to your faith in Christ. And He is on the track with you now, empowering you by the Holy Spirit to keep reaching forward. You simply must cooperate with His plan for finishing the race. What can you do to cooperate? We'll be talking more about that in part 3.

Even if your walk with Christ has been severely hindered by one or more of the risk factors we have mentioned, don't give up the race. It's not too late. Grab hold of God's hope-filled promises, and run to win.

The health of your spiritual heart and your physical heart depends on what you feed them. In the next two chapters, Drs. Duncan and Leachman will unmask one of the primary enemies of the physical heart: the problem of eating too much.

Chapter 6: Ominous Signs
of Spiritual Heart Disease

- Just as there are risk factors threatening physical heart health, so there are risk factors threatening the health of the spiritual heart:

  1. *Family history.* The key to overcoming a painful family history is to focus on who you are instead of who you were. Healing comes when you recognize that Christ has put you in a new family.

  2. *Spiritual deafness.* God will help you overcome spiritual heart disease if you heed His strategies. But if you neglect Him and wander far from His call, there will be a sad payoff.

  3. *Spiritual malnutrition.* If you're not eating right spiritually, you will lack the power to resist temptation and grow strong. You must feed daily on Christ and His Word.

  4. *Lack of spiritual exercise.* Energy balance—energy in, energy out—is as important to spiritual vitality as it is to physical vitality. Find ways to serve God by serving others.

  5. *Fear of failure.* Many Christians never leave the starting line because they are paralyzed by the fear of failure. Overcome the fear of failure by not looking backward but pressing forward.

- If you want to successfully confront and neutralize the risk factors for spiritual heart disease, you need to be a man of hope.

7

As Your Stomach Goes, So Goes Your Heart

What you don't know about what you eat can literally kill you.

Dr. Michael Duncan and Dr. Richard Leachman

It's difficult to avoid being swept up in our culture's obsession with food. God designed the human body in such a way that we must *eat to live*. We cannot operate without fuel—the air we breathe and the food and liquids we consume. The tragedy of anorexia in our culture demonstrates what happens when someone refuses to eat. But our culture is bombarded today with the twisted, appealing, and convincing message that we must *live to eat*. And the difference in how these three little words are arranged can literally kill you.

By God's marvelous design, if you eat the right kinds of foods in appropriate quantities, you will maximize your opportunities to live a long, healthy, and productive life. You can work into your sixties or seventies if you want and still have a couple of decades for the fun of retirement. Make plans to dance at the weddings of your grandchildren—maybe even your great-grandchildren! All you have to do is keep your heart humming along at maximum efficiency with the right fuel and care.

But it is difficult to maintain a sane eat-to-live program in a food-crazed, live-to-eat society. Enjoyment in life is so often equated with food—good food, rich food, piles of food. We're attracted to "man-sized" meals and all-you-can-eat night at the restaurant, which is usually more food than the average man should eat in one sitting. The employee at the fast-food counter asks, "Would you like to super-size your meal for only fifty cents more?" Food ads on TV push taste, convenience, quantity, and value (more calories and fat for less money) over nutrition.

Quantity is the most common problem for men today regarding food. When you eat, your body turns the food into energy and then burns that energy through your daily activity. When you put more fuel energy into your system than you can immediately use, your body holds the residual in ready reserve and uses it if fuel intake is low. But when you consistently take in more fuel than you burn and your reserves are full, the body must find a place to store the excess. Medically speaking, that storage facility is called adipose tissue, which is located throughout your body. In unflattering layperson's terms, this tissue may be described as a "spare tire" or "love handles." According to bodybuilder-turned-politician Arnold Schwarzenegger, "It's simple. If it jiggles, it's fat."

A healthy body burns fuel and stores fuel in reserve. The main form of fuel storage in the body is fat. For the typical 170-pound man, roughly 20 percent of body weight—about thirty-four pounds—is fat. Statistically, most of us carry more than that. Fuel storage assures that you will be able to survive and function for a time even when you are unable to eat or choose not to eat through a fast. But excessive fuel storage over the long haul taxes the body, precipitates disease, and shortens life.

The live-to-eat perversion in our country has reached epidemic proportions. We are experiencing a medical crisis that is literally killing us. The epidemic is obesity, the sad and dangerous result of falling prey to the live-to-eat lie in our culture. Obesity is the most common metabolic disorder in the Western world. The American Obesity Association Web site reports that 64.5 percent of adult Americans (about 127 million) are categorized as being overweight or obese.[1] Furthermore, sixty million Americans are clinically obese, and nine million are severely obese.[2]

Body Mass Index: Your Weight-to-Height Ratio

One of the helpful tools for determining how much weight is too much is called the body mass index (BMI). Years of obesity research have helped us determine a healthy range for a person's weight in proportion to his height. Simply put, your height is a reliable standard for determining how much you can weigh and still be within the margin of good health.

You calculate BMI using the following formula:

> Your weight in pounds
> divided by your height in inches squared
> multiplied by a factor of 703

For example, let's calculate the BMI of two men with the same height. Joe stands 5'10" (70 inches) and weighs 170 pounds.

> Joe's height in inches squared (70 x 70) equals 4,900.
> His weight in pounds (170) divided by 4,900 equals 0.035.
> 0.035 times 703 equals a BMI of 24.6.

Charlie also stands 5'10" but weighs 200 pounds.

> Charlie's height in inches squared (70 x 70) equals 4,900.
> His weight in pounds (200) divided by 4,900 equals 0.041.
> 0.041 times 703 equals a BMI of 28.8.

Overweight is clinically defined as a body mass index of 25 or greater. *Obesity* is clinically defined as a BMI of 30 or greater. A BMI of 40 or greater indicates *severe obesity*, also called *morbid obesity*. Numerous studies have shown that a BMI above 25 increases a person's risk of dying early, mainly from heart disease and cancer. Conversely, death rates decline when the BMI is within the safe range.

Joe, with a BMI just under 25, is inside the safe range, just short of being overweight for his height. Charlie's BMI of 28.8 puts him at the borderline between overweight and obesity and at higher risk than Joe for heart disease, related problems, and earlier death. The following chart will help you quickly identify the weight range that is safe for your height.

Height (in.)	Weight (lb.)													
58	91	96	100	105	110	115	119	124	129	134	138	143	167	191
59	94	99	104	109	114	119	124	128	133	138	143	148	173	198
60	97	102	107	112	118	123	128	133	138	143	148	153	179	204
61	100	106	111	116	122	127	132	137	143	148	153	158	185	211
62	104	109	115	120	126	131	136	142	147	153	158	164	191	218
63	107	113	118	124	130	135	141	146	152	158	163	169	197	225
64	110	116	122	128	134	140	145	151	157	163	169	174	204	232
65	114	120	126	132	138	144	150	156	162	168	174	180	210	240
66	118	124	130	136	142	148	155	161	167	173	179	186	216	247
67	121	127	134	140	146	153	159	166	172	178	185	191	223	255
68	125	131	138	144	151	158	164	171	177	184	190	197	230	262
69	128	135	142	149	155	162	169	176	182	189	196	203	236	270
70	132	139	146	153	160	167	174	181	188	195	202	207	243	276
71	136	143	150	157	165	172	179	186	193	200	208	215	250	286
72	140	147	154	162	169	177	184	191	199	206	213	221	258	294
73	144	151	159	166	174	182	189	197	204	212	219	227	265	302
74	148	155	163	171	179	186	194	202	210	218	225	233	272	311
75	152	160	168	176	184	192	200	208	216	224	232	240	279	319
76	156	164	172	180	189	197	205	213	221	230	238	246	287	328
BMI	19	20	21	22	23	24	25	26	27	28	29	30	35	40

Tipping the Scales: A National Epidemic

It is sobering to note that the prevalence of clinically overweight and obese persons in our country has increased dramatically during the past three decades and especially in the last several years. This disturbing and dangerous trend has affected all age groups of both genders, as the following tables prepared by the American Obesity Association indicate.

The first table on page 69 reports the rise in the number of overweight, obese, and severely obese men and women between two statistical periods: 1988–1994 and 1999–2000. For example, you can see that the prevalence of overweight men in the United States rose from 61 percent to 67 percent between the two periods, indicating that 67 percent of all American men in 1999–2000 were clinically overweight.[3]

	Men Prevalence (%)		Women Prevalence (%)	
	1988–1994	1999–2000	1988–1994	1999–2000
Overweight BMI 25 or greater	61	67	51.2	62
Obese BMI 30 or greater	20.6	27.7	26	34
Severely Obese BMI 40 or greater	1.7	3.12	4	6.3

The table below breaks down the rise in overweight prevalence into age categories for men and women. Note, for example, that 58 percent of men ages twenty-two to thirty-four were overweight in 1999–2000, as compared to 47.5 percent in 1988–1994—an increase of more than 10 percentage points.[4]

Overweight (BMI 25 or greater)

	Men Prevalence (%)		Women Prevalence (%)	
Age (Years)	1988–1994	1999–2000	1988–1994	1999–2000
22–34	47.5	58.0	37.0	51.5
35–44	65.5	67.6	49.6	63.6
45–54	66.1	71.3	60.3	64.7
55–64	70.5	72.5	66.3	73.1
65–74	68.5	77.2	60.3	70.1
75+	56.5	66.4	52.3	59.6

The table below reflects the increase in prevalence of obesity between the two statistical periods by age groups. Notice that obesity across the board increased, just as numbers for overweight men increased in every age category.[5]

Obese (BMI 30 or greater)

Age (Years)	Men Prevalence (%)		Women Prevalence (%)	
	1988–1994	1999–2000	1988–1994	1999–2000
22–34	14.1	24.1	18.5	25.8
35–44	21.5	25.2	25.5	33.9
45–54	23.2	30.1	32.4	38.1
55–64	27.2	32.9	33.7	43.1
65–74	24.1	33.4	26.9	38.8
75+	13.2	20.4	19.2	25.1

In the U.S. alone, three hundred thousand deaths annually are directly related to obesity, costing an estimated $100 billion.[6] This deadly rise has occurred despite all the information about the dangers of being overweight and obese. No, we don't see boldly printed warnings from the surgeon general on hamburger wrappers, ice-cream cartons, and menus at the doughnut shop like we do on cigarette packs. But who hasn't been informed or sternly warned by someone in the healthcare community that being overweight or obese increases our risk of a wide array of medical problems, any of which can hit the fast-forward button on the timetable of our death?

The Slippery Slope of Being Overweight

Exactly what are these problems? Where can being overweight or obese lead? Here are a number of places you don't want to go physically, dangerous destinations along the slippery slope of eating for pleasure and convenience instead of health.

Coronary artery disease (CAD). This is the condition produced by the buildup of plaque in the arteries that carry blood to the heart muscles. As heart specialists, we see some form of CAD every day, often in patients who are overweight or obese. They are heart attacks waiting to happen. CAD patients come in with blockages in their coronary arteries, in need of bypass surgery or stents to prevent heart attack.

Stroke. Stroke results when one of the arteries supplying blood to the brain becomes narrowed or blocked, often by plaque or hardening of the arteries.

Diabetes. Approximately 75 percent of all patients with Type II diabetes are also overweight or obese.

Hypertension. For the person who is obese, hypertension—high blood pressure—is very common. Being overweight or obese can trigger hypertension.

Hyperlipidemia and high cholesterol. The buildup of fats and cholesterol in the bloodstream is directly linked to being overweight or obese.

Osteoarthritis. Degenerative joint disease, or osteoarthritis, develops as the body wears down under excessive weight, and the ankles, knees, and hips begin to deteriorate under the pressure. It is not uncommon to find obese people age fifty or younger coming in for bilateral knee and/or hip replacement, severely limiting mobility or sentencing them to a wheelchair.

Cancer. Obesity has been linked to specific types of kidney cancer, colon cancer, and, in women, postmenopausal breast cancer and endometrial cancer.

Sleep apnea. Think about the last time you were x-rayed at the dentist. Remember wearing that heavy lead "apron" that protected your vital organs from the x-rays? Did you notice that it impaired your breathing somewhat simply because of the extra weight? That's what sleep apnea does, a breathing disorder characterized by brief interruptions of breathing during sleep. Being overweight or obese is like wearing a lead apron all the time, restricting and interrupting breathing.

Gallstones. Gallstones are clusters of solid material, made mostly from cholesterol, that form in the gallbladder and can cause severe disease as a result of acute inflammation. Being overweight or obese, which is often linked to high levels of cholesterol, is a definite contributor to gallstones.

Gout. Gout is a very painful disease caused by an elevated level of uric acid in the bloodstream. When the level becomes too high, crystals of uric acid form in various joints in the body, causing intense inflammation. Gout has a much higher incidence in patients who are overweight or obese.

Getting Your Weight Back in Balance

Here are three health axioms that will, if heeded, dramatically diminish your risk of developing any of these many problems. These axioms are stated by Dr. Walter Willett in his excellent book, *Eat, Drink, and Be Healthy.*[7]

Next to smoking, your weight is the most important measure of your future health. Your BMI identifies a safe weight range for your height. You may look at the chart and exclaim, "I haven't been at that weight since my first year in college!" Don't let that number be a tyrant in your life. Total Heart Health is about embracing a lifestyle that will keep you moving toward your weight goals instead of drifting away from a healthy weight range. The apostle Paul spoke about finishing the course laid out for him in the face of many obstacles (see 2 Timothy 4:7). You might not fit into your ROTC uniform or the tux you wore to the senior prom anymore, but every step in that direction, no matter how small, is a positive step toward a healthier, longer life. Stay in the race and finish well.

Limiting daily calorie intake is the single most important strategy for controlling weight. Calories supply the energy our bodies need to function. We gain energy by eating, because food contains calories. We expend energy through activity, because everything we do burns calories. The math is very simple. If you take in more calories than you burn, the unused calories are stored as fat and you gain weight. But if you take in fewer calories than you use up, your body burns some of your stored fat for energy and you lose weight.

We call this "energy balance": total daily energy (calories) consumed minus total daily energy expended. If you want to maintain your weight, the numbers on both sides of this equation must be roughly equal—you must burn off about what you take in. But if you want to lose weight, you must burn more energy than you take in.

The recommendations for controlling weight that we present in this book infer that you will keep tabs on the number of calories you consume. That's right, men, calorie counting isn't just for women; it's important for anyone who wants a healthy heart. You don't have to tote a calculator to the meal table at home and to a restaurant when you eat out. Instead, you just need a good working knowledge of the approximate calorie count in what you eat. Calorie-counting booklets are available at your local bookstore.

There's no way around it: weight loss and weight control require your active participation, and buying into our recommendations means tracking daily calorie intake. You must also know how many daily calories you need to maintain your level of activity.

A healthy diet, combined with regular exercise and no smoking, can eliminate 80 percent of heart disease and 70 percent of some cancers. This is a marvelous pay-off, isn't it? Give care to diet and exercise, and your odds soar for a longer, healthier life in which to serve God, help people, and enjoy life. This is an achievable outcome because weight control is a doable activity for any man. We're going to coach you to eat foods that are good for you and to avoid the foods that adversely affect your health. And if you need to start losing weight, we have provided a 21-day, low-calorie menu plan in chapter 20 that you can follow as is or adapt to your lifestyle.

Combining healthy calorie intake (energy in) and healthy calorie expenditure (energy out) leads to a healthy life. In the next chapter, we will talk about the energy-out side of the equation.

Chapter 7: As Your Stomach Goes,
So Goes Your Heart

- God designed the human body in such a way that we must *eat to live,* but our culture is bombarded with the twisted, appealing, and convincing message that we must *live to eat.*

- If you eat the right kinds of foods in appropriate quantities, you will maximize your opportunities to live a long, healthy, productive life.

- Quantity is the most common problem for men today regarding food.

- One of the most helpful tools for determining how much weight is too much is the body mass index (BMI). A BMI of 25 or greater indicates a person is overweight, 30 or greater indicates obesity, and 40 or greater indicates morbid obesity.

- Being obese or overweight can lead to coronary heart disease, stroke, diabetes, hypertension, hyperlipidemia and high cholesterol, cancer, sleep apnea, gallstones, and gout.

- Three health axioms that will diminish your health risk:

  1. Next to smoking, your weight is the most important measure of your future health.

  2. Limiting daily calorie intake is the single most important strategy for controlling weight.

  3. A healthy diet, combined with regular exercise and no smoking, can eliminate 80 percent of heart disease and 70 percent of some cancers.

Are the Calories You Eat Working for You or Against You?

Counting calories is as good for you as
for the women in your life.

Dr. Michael Duncan and Dr. Richard Leachman

We need calories to live, so we must eat calories every day. Calories are utilized as energy for everything we do. How much energy is in a calorie? Scientifically speaking, one calorie is the amount of energy needed to raise the temperature of one liter of water by one degree centigrade (1° C). On a more practical level, a 150-pound man will burn up approximately 480 calories during eight hours of sleep. That's right, you are burning up calories every moment you're alive, even when you are sleeping. What a great way to lose weight! It's just that you're not burning up very many calories during sleep compared to the calories you take in when you're awake.

So the big question is, how much energy—in other words, how many calories—do you need each day to maintain a healthy life? There is no magic number of calories that fits every person. Daily caloric needs are different for each of us depending on height, weight, gender, age, and activity level. So you need to determine what we call your individual calorie-need profile.

Focusing on the Calories You Need

Your calorie-need profile takes into account two factors: your basal metabolic rate and the intensity of your weekly physical activity.

Basal Metabolic Rate

Your basal metabolic rate (BMR) measures the amount of calorie fuel your body requires just to keep you alive with all your organs functioning. Most diets allow more calories for men than for women because men tend to have a higher BMR than women, meaning men burn more calories. Women usually have a higher BMR during pregnancy and lactation because these stages require more energy.

Children and youth have a very high BMR to fuel their growth. That's why most growing, active kids can load up on pizza and burgers and doughnuts and soda without putting on much weight. They burn up calories like a dragster burns up fuel. But as an adult, you don't need as much calorie fuel to maintain life. Whenever we eat like teenagers, we usually end up paying for it with extra pounds. And from midlife on, it seems we don't need to eat much at all to maintain ideal body weight.

Like your BMI, your BMR requires a simple calculation: body weight in kilograms times 24. To determine your weight in kilograms, divide your weight in pounds by 2.2, then multiply your kilogram weight by 24 to arrive at your BMR—the daily number of calories your body requires to maintain life. For example, Jack's weight of 165 pounds translates to 75 kilograms. Multiplied by 24, his weight in kilograms equates to a BMR of 1,800. So Jack needs an average of 1,800 calories each day just to live.

But the *B* in BMR stands for *basal*, meaning it is only the starting point. BMR quantifies the needs of a man who is completely sedentary—no exercise, no activity, just living and breathing, heart beating, kidneys and liver functioning. Unless Jack is in a coma or is a total invalid, he needs more than 1,800 calories a day. In addition to his BMR, he needs enough calories to adequately fuel all his activities—and so do you.

Activity Level

The other element for determining your calorie-need profile is your activity level. You must add to your BMR the number of calories you burn for the activity level of your daily life. For example, Reggie leads a very active life. Working forty hours a week as a stonemason, he is on the go all day long—a lot of ladder climbing and heavy lifting. Reggie also plays in a volleyball league at the local YMCA. So he is working out, practicing, or playing matches three to four evenings each week. His moderate to high activity level six days a week requires a lot of calorie fuel, almost double that of his BMR. So let's multiply Reggie's BMR by 1.8, pushing his average daily calorie-need profile to around 3,300. This is the approximate number of calories Reggie needs to live and stay active at his level.

By comparison, let's talk about Irwin, a seventy-two-year-old man who lives with his wife in a retirement complex. Irwin also weighs 165 pounds, giving him a BMR equal to Reggie's: 1,800. But Irwin's activity level is significantly lower than Reggie's. On a typical day, Irwin rises to eat breakfast, read the newspaper, watch the morning news, and take the couple's two little dogs for a walk. After lunch, Irwin sits down at the computer to track their investments, then he often lies down on the sofa for a nap. Most evenings, Irwin and Winnie take a little stroll with the dogs after dinner, then they settle in to watch their favorite TV programs.

Irwin's relatively low activity level requires significantly fewer calories than Reggie's, perhaps a third of his BMR. Multiplying Irwin's BMR of 1,800 by 1.3, we see that his daily calorie-need profile is in the 2,300 range.

Your calorie-need profile likely falls somewhere between that of a retiree like Irwin and a racecar like Reggie. The chart below will help you approximate how many calories you burn in your daily activities. The more strenuous the activity, the more calories you use. Add that number to your BMR, and you have your calorie-need profile—a rough idea of the calorie energy your body needs each day.

Type of Exercise	Calories/Hour	Type of Exercise	Calories/Hour	Type of Exercise	Calories/Hour
Sleeping	55	Dancing, ballroom	260	Swimming, active	500+
Eating	85	Walking, 3 mph	280	Cross-country ski machine	500+
Sewing	85	Tennis	350+	Hiking	500+
Sitting	85	Water aerobics	400	Step aerobics	550+
Standing	100	Skating/Rollerblading	420+	Rowing	550+
Office work	140	Dancing/aerobic	420+	Power walking	600+
Housework, moderate	160+	Aerobics	450+	Cycling, studio	650
Golf, with cart	180	Bicycling, moderate	450+	Skipping with rope	700+
Golf, without cart	240	Jogging, 5 mph	500	Running	700+
Gardening, planting	250	Gardening, digging	500		

Making Calories Play by Your Rules

Here's the bottom line to your calorie-need profile: if your profile is roughly equal to the number of calories you take in, your weight will remain about the same week in and week out. You are in what we call energy balance: your energy out is about the same as your energy in. However, if your calorie intake is greater than your profile, you will gain weight because the surplus will be stored as fat. But if you take in fewer calories than your profile, you will lose weight because your body burns off the surplus to compensate for the calorie deficit. Weight loss is as simple as that.

How great a calorie deficit do you need to shed pounds? It might be helpful to know that there are 3,500 calories in one pound of fat. So to lose one pound, you need a calorie deficit of 3,500 calories—meaning your energy out must exceed your energy in by 3,500 calories. Theoretically, if you manage a calorie deficit of 3,500 calories each day, you would lose one pound a day. But we're not in favor of such crash programs—because the "crash" could hurt you more than it helps. We have a more sensible approach in mind.

Here's what we recommend. If your calorie-need profile is somewhere between Reggie's and Irwin's—roughly 2,800 calories—and you want to gradually shed pounds, try a 1,000-calorie-per-day deficit. In other words, instead of maintaining energy balance at 2,800 calories, limit your daily intake to around 1,800 calories. At 1,000 calories per day, your weekly deficit will be 7,000 calories. And since there are 3,500 calories in a pound of fat, you could lose about two pounds a week.

Now two pounds in seven days may seem rather boring compared to the outrageous claims made by some of the fad weight-loss programs on the market. But it is a realistic, safe, and relatively painless way to take off unwanted pounds. Think about it: at two pounds a week, a severely obese person can lose 104 pounds during the course of a year. Think what you can do in a year! Simply adopt a healthy, balanced weekly menu that fits within your daily target calorie count, and watch the pounds and inches slip away.

If your daily calorie-need profile is closer to that of a very active Reggie at 3,300, you may want to try a 1,500-calorie deficit to lose weight faster. But for someone like Irwin, whose profile is much lower, a 1,000-calorie deficit may be too harsh. You may want to back off to a 700- to 800-calorie deficit. The pounds will come off more slowly, but as long as you operate in deficit mode, you will lose weight.

How to Succeed at Weight Control

Losing weight, even a pound or two a month, is a challenge. And keeping the pounds off is an even greater challenge. But a ten-year study called the National Weight Control Registry provides encouragement and hope that you can achieve and maintain your weight-loss goals.[1] More than four thousand people have participated in the study. Here are a few insights gained from the findings.

Stop Gaining Weight

Most people in America are gaining weight, so if you can neutralize weight gain, you are ahead of the curve and should feel a measure of success.[2] Perhaps an intermediate weight-loss goal for you is to achieve energy balance—eliminating further weight gain. You should feel some satisfaction about staying at the same pant size for a year or more and getting more mileage out of your wardrobe.

Proceed with Small, Manageable Goals

When you're ready to lose some pounds, studies show that you are more likely to succeed if you take small steps. For example, here is a man whose body mass index is a very unhealthy 38. He needs to lose at least eighty pounds to reverse the damage his obesity is wreaking in his body. But losing eighty pounds is an extremely daunting goal, like climbing Mount Everest might be to a novice mountain climber. However, losing fifteen to twenty pounds and maintaining that loss is manageable for most people. By reaching a modest goal, this obese man will be more confident and hopeful about beginning his next campaign to take off another fifteen to twenty pounds.

Play the Weight-Loss Percentages

Successful weight loss is defined as losing 10 percent of your initial body weight and not regaining it. In other words, it is better to lose ten pounds and keep it off than to lose twenty pounds, gain it back, and then lose it again. Using this definition, only 20 percent of the participants in the study were termed "successful" because the others could not keep from regaining the weight loss. There were two main behavioral reasons for this lack of success. First, the study found that these people focused too much on diet and not enough on exercise. Second, they focused on losing the weight but not on keeping it off.

Diet and Exercise

In the study, there was no dominant motive and no dominant diet and exercise plan for successful weight loss. Some people entered the study to improve health, some to look better, others to feel better, still others to build self-esteem. And the diet plans and exercise regimens employed were all over the map. But there was one clearly common approach to losing weight: 89 percent of those who succeeded did so through diet and exercise. Only 10 percent of the participants succeeded using diet alone, and barely 1 percent lost weight using exercise alone. It's hard to argue with success.

Here are several common factors of diet and exercise for those in the study who succeeded in reaching and maintaining their weight goals:

Participants averaged 1,300 to 1,500 calories per day consumed. Compare this to the national average of 3,500 calories consumed per day. This is why most people across the country are gaining weight. The weight-loss menu plan we provide in chapter 20 provides approximately 1,600 calories per day.

All ate breakfast regularly. Many people mistakenly believe that skipping breakfast is the way to lose weight. This study suggests otherwise. Eating a nutritious breakfast can help jump-start your metabolism for burning calories all day long.

Seventy-five percent weighed themselves regularly, either daily or weekly. We believe consistent weigh-ins—at least weekly—are important. You need to check your weight often to make sure your program is working. If you are not losing weight, there's something wrong with your diet math. Either you're taking in too many calories or you're not burning off enough calories.

All participated in extensive physical activity. People burned an average of 2,500 calories per day through basal metabolic rate and sixty to ninety minutes of moderate to intense exercise. However, in most cases, participants in the study weren't on a jogging track or a treadmill for sixty to ninety minutes a day. Rather, they counted some of their daily activity as calorie-burning exercise.

For example, many participants in the study wore pedometers—small devices that clip to a belt and count your steps. Those who did a lot of walking during the day counted it as part of their exercise. For example, twelve thousand steps translate into six miles of walking, which burns about six hundred calories. When it comes to cardio exercise, it is preferable to sustain physical activity over a certain time period, like forty minutes of jogging or swimming laps. But for burning calories, all your activities count toward your daily target.

Our Total Heart Health recommendation for every man is at least thirty minutes of moderate exercise six days per week. Walking is a good example. You can cover about two miles in thirty minutes of brisk walking. At 100 calories a mile, you will burn 200 calories a day, 1,200 calories a week, and 62,400 calories a year. And since one pound of fat equates to 3,500 calories, you could potentially lose about eighteen pounds a year just from eating right and walking two miles a day.

Diet? Me? You've Got to Be Kidding

The importance of monitoring calorie intake brings us to the "D word"—*diet*. Most men have tried at least one form of dieting, and most dieters have experienced the frustration of "falling off the wagon" and failing to accomplish their dieting goals. The late comedian Jackie Gleason, of *The Honeymooners* fame, once quipped, "The second day of a diet is always easier. By the second day you're off it." Calories and carbs, protein and portions, fats and fasting—they all get so confusing. For many men today, *diet* is right up there with other four-letter words we avoid uttering. It seems like weight-control plans are the enemy of a healthy heart instead of a friend.

Why don't diets work? Here are three common answers we hear from people.

"Diets Are Boring"

Many men complain that the list of foods they *can't* eat on a diet is much longer than the list of foods they *can* eat. After a couple of weeks of the "same old, same old," they lose interest. Life is too short for salads and rice cakes five times a week. Or as *Garfield* cartoonist Jim Davis wrote, "Vegetables are a must on a diet. I suggest carrot cake, zucchini bread, and pumpkin pie."

Our Total Heart Health recommendations include all food groups. We will give you tips on how to navigate through the options to find the foods and portions that are best while steering clear of foods that are clearly detrimental to heart health. The three-week menu of healthy meals we provide in chapter 20 is designed to help you lose weight. Before launching into a new diet plan, especially when it calls for a big change in your calorie intake, talk to your doctor.

"When I'm on a Diet, I'm Always Hungry"

The sensation of hunger has a lot to do with blood-sugar level. When your blood sugar takes a dive, your body insists, *I'm starving; let's eat!* We'll talk later about glycemic index and show you how to avoid riding the blood-sugar roller coaster, which so often sends you scurrying to the fridge at home or the vending machine at work for a snack.

Obviously, hunger also occurs when the stomach shrinks while emptying, and hunger is satisfied when the stomach is full. We will show you the kinds of food that slow down stomach emptying and nutrient absorption so you feel fuller longer.

"If There Are Cookies or Potato Chips in the House, I Can't Be Trusted"

Exerting self-control in what we eat is not just about food; it's clearly a total heart issue that applies to all of life. The apostle Paul lamented, "I decide to do good, but I don't *really* do it; I decide not to do bad, but then I do it anyway" (Romans 7:19 MSG). Doesn't that sound like the very dilemma we face when trying to choose something healthy from a menu of mouth-watering choices at the local restaurant?

Self-control is an issue of the spiritual heart as much as the physical heart. Paul wrote, "The flesh sets its desire against the Spirit, and the Spirit against the flesh; for these are in opposition to one another, so that you may not do the things that you please" (Galatians 5:17). But then he brings us the good news: "Those who belong to Christ Jesus have crucified the flesh with its passions and desires" (v. 24).

This is why we have teamed with our pastor to write this book about Total Heart Health. As we have been saying, you can't segment your heart into categories—physical, spiritual, emotional, intellectual. You are a whole person, and each facet of the whole impacts the other facets. The self-discipline you need for establishing healthy habits in your physical life springs from your spiritual life. The chapters provided by Dr. Young are helping you grow in spiritual heart health as we encourage and implement the health of your physical heart. The more you build up the spiritual heart muscle, the more it can help you strengthen your physical heart.

Your physical heart is a target for destruction. Drs. Duncan and Leachman will now expose lethal myths about food and diet that are aimed at weakening your heart and robbing you of vitality.

Chapter 8: Are the Calories You Eat Working for You or Against You?

- How many calories do you need each day to maintain a healthy life? Your calorie-need profile takes into account two factors: your basal metabolic rate (BMR) and the intensity of your weekly physical activity.

- Your BMR measures the amount of calorie fuel your body requires just to keep you alive with all the organs functioning.

- To find your daily calorie-need profile, add to your BMR the number of calories you burn for the activity level of your daily life.

- If your profile is roughly equal to the number of calories you take in, your weight will remain about the same. If your calorie intake is greater than your profile, you will gain weight. If you take in fewer calories than your profile, you will lose weight.

- Diets don't work when people find them boring, so our Total Heart Health recommendations include all food groups.

- Diets don't work when dieters always feel hungry, so our plan shows you the kinds of food that slow down stomach emptying and nutrient absorption so you feel fuller longer.

- Diets don't work when people don't exercise self-control, and that's an issue of the spiritual heart as much as the physical heart.

9

Diet and Exercise Trends You Don't Want to Follow

Four areas where "keeping up with the Joneses" can hurt your heart.

Dr. Michael Duncan and Dr. Richard Leachman

You pull up to the red light in your two-year-old sedan, which you bought brand-new. It's a really nice car. It has everything you wanted—color, upholstery, extras, and a fantastic sound system. And you got a great deal on the car. But . . . it's a sedan.

Sitting next to you at the light is a guy in the newest-model SUV to hit the market. It looks so cool! And it has standard features that weren't even offered as options when you got your sedan. Before the light turns green, you see three more late-model SUVs drive past you. One of them looked like your brother-in-law's rig. Waiting for the light to turn green, you can think of four other guys you know who recently traded in their sedans or coupes for SUVs. There's not a thing wrong with your sedan, but it wouldn't hurt anything to stop by the SUV dealer and kick the tires on one of those beauties.

You've been there, right? If it wasn't a fascination with a new trend in cars, you have probably noticed something else that's new, different, and desirable: the latest in men's clothes or a new generation in home-theater systems, golf clubs, or power tools. These trends catch you up in what it seems everybody is doing. And since nobody likes to be left out, you feel that tug to join in the flow.

There are also trends when it comes to physical health. During the past several decades, there has been a fair amount of evolution in our country's approach to diet and exercise. Medical authorities, including some of the national medical societies, continue to update health recommendations to reflect concerns about health issues, especially coronary artery disease and heart disease in general, the number one killer in the United States. And along with these recommendations come many popular trends for how we should take care of our bodies.

Trading in your sedan for that truck or SUV everybody else seems to have isn't likely to affect your physical health. Nor will it be a health issue when you swap out your woods and irons for the popular new brand or style. But trying to keep up with some of the popular trends in diet and exercise *can* be harmful to your health. Here are four such trends that should be approached with caution because of the possible negative impact on your heart health.

Trend 1: Forgo All Fats

As it became clear that abnormal cholesterol levels in the bloodstream are a risk factor in developing heart disease, the American Heart Association and other national health authorities recommended that patients should follow a diet low in fat—particularly saturated fat—and cholesterol. Most doctors around the country passed these recommendations along to their patients and to the general public. As a result, a popular health trend has gained wide acceptance: *all fats are bad, so we should exclude fat from our diet.*

How has this trend taken hold in our culture? An entire food industry has grown up around this trend. You can see it every time you go into the super-market. Notice how many food products on the shelf are labeled "fat-free," "nonfat," "low-fat," "reduced fat," "less fat," "lite," and so on. You can also see it every time you go out to eat. Many restaurants today highlight menu items that are low in fat and considered healthier for the heart. Be honest now: when you go out for lunch, don't you at least consider the option of ordering a big salad—with fat-free dressing—instead of a burger and fries?

As doctors, we have a couple of problems with the trend to forgo all fats. First, we disagree with the assumption that all fats are bad, because this assumption is false. Dietary fat in proper amounts is essential for normal body health because fat is a necessary component of cell membranes in the body. Fat regulates and facilitates the production, distribution, and function of good cholesterol. It is involved in the absorption and distribution of fat-soluble vitamins including D, E, A, and K. Fat is important in the insulation of nerves and aids in nerve conduction. Fat is present to a large degree in the brain and is part of normal brain function.

Fat—in the form of adipose tissue—is the major fuel storage component of our bodies. We all need a certain amount of adipose tissue to insulate the body against extreme temperatures, to cushion the vital organs, and to store potential energy. Consequently, not all fats are bad. In fact, being swept along by this trend to avoid all fatty foods like the plague may even negatively affect your health.

Another problem we see with this trend is the built-in temptation to eat more. For example, you bring home from the market reduced-fat ice cream or low-fat sandwich spread or "lite" salad dressing. Since these products are "healthier," you tend to serve larger portions of them. You think, *It's not as bad for me, so I can eat more of it.* By upping our portion sizes in this way, we not only cancel out some of the benefits of lowering fat consumption, but we also tend to eat more overall calories.

We will talk about the proper balance of fats in the diet when we get to chapter 12, which covers the three primary dietary fuels: fats, carbohydrates, and protein.

Trend 2: Cancel Out Carbs

As the trend to avoid fats grew, where did people turn to fill up the empty space on their dinner plates? To carbohydrates. They cut back on fatty red meats and piled on more "harmless" potatoes and breads, prompting the health community to issue new warnings about eating carbs in relatively unlimited quantities. This warning has given rise to a carb-conscious trend, carving out another new niche in the food industry: carb-free and low-carb foods. We adopted the mind-set that carbohydrates are as bad for us as fats, so we'd better cancel them out of our diet too.

The anti-carb trend opened the door for numerous low-carbohydrate diets, some of which are very popular—the Atkins Diet and the Sugar Busters Diet, among others. These dietary plans correctly point out that some types of carbohydrates, particularly simple carbohydrates, can be metabolized into the bloodstream quite rapidly, resulting in wide swings in blood sugar levels. The low-carb or carb-free diets are aimed at controlling high spikes in blood sugar that tend to encourage overeating and weight gain.

The biology of rapidly metabolized simple carbohydrates is reflected in what is called the *glycemic index*. This index shows how quickly the carbohydrates in certain foods are broken down into glucose and enter the bloodstream to elevate blood sugar. Foods with a high glycemic index cause a rapid rise in blood sugar, and foods with a low glycemic index prompt a slower rise in blood sugar. The overall desired response is for blood sugar to rise gradually and fall gradually. This response is achieved by consuming fewer foods known to have a high glycemic index.

The carbohydrates that most need to be controlled are known as simple carbohydrates, also called simple sugars. Simple carbs are those that are more easily broken down during digestion. Complex carbohydrates take longer to break down, so the rise in blood sugar is more gradual. Here's a good example of the two. When you drink a glass of apple juice (simple carbohydrate), it will hit your system fast and spike your blood sugar to a high level very quickly. But if you eat an apple (complex carbohydrate), your system takes longer to digest it, resulting in a much more gradual rise in blood sugar.

Refined foods such as white breads, pastries, packaged cookies, and cakes have a high glycemic index. This is because the refining process eliminates the bran and germ components from the wheat kernel, leaving only the endosperm and the white flour, which essentially jump-start the digestive process. Wheat germ has B complex vitamins, vitamin E, and trace minerals. Wheat bran is a great source of fiber, and both elements have high quantities of B vitamins and other micronutrients. The endosperm has much less nutritive value and is a simple carbohydrate quickly metabolized to produce high blood sugar. This is why whole-grain products are much better for you than refined products. The chart on page 89 provides a sampling of foods categorized from very low to very high on the glycemic index.

Why is this important? Let's say you gulp down a jelly sandwich on white bread, a twelve-ounce can of sugary soda, and a candy bar for lunch—a meal that is loaded with simple sugars. Your blood sugar will soon skyrocket, prompting your pancreas to secrete insulin into the bloodstream to capture

Glycemic Index of Certain Foods

Food	Index	Food	Index	Food	Index
Artificial sweeteners	>5	Orange juice	52	Potato, mashed	70
Diet soda, without caffeine	0	Bananas	54	Tortilla, corn	70
Grapefruit	25	Sweet potato	54	Bagel, white	72
Whole milk	27	Rice, brown	55	Watermelon	72
Butter beans	31	Sweet corn	55	Cheerios	74
Lima beans	32	Honey	58	Graham crackers	74
Skim milk	32	Rice, white	58	Potato, French fries	75
Apples	38	Cheese pizza	60	Doughnuts, plain	76
Tomato soup	38	Hamburger bun	61	Vanilla wafers	77
Pinto beans	39	Ice cream	61	White bread	78
Snickers bar	40	Oatmeal, quick	61	Pretzels	81
Spaghetti, white	41	Black bean soup	64	Rice Krispies	82
Oranges	44	Chocolate chip cookies	64	Cornflakes	83
Linguini	46	Macaroni & cheese	64	Potato, baked	85
Grapefruit juice	48	Raisins	64	Rice, white, instant	90
Carrots	49	Sucrose (table sugar)	64	Gatorade	95
Oatmeal, regular	49	Soft drinks	68	Glucose	100

this sugar and use it for energy. As the blood sugar continues to surge, the insulin goes into high gear and drives the blood sugar way down to keep it under control. When blood sugar plummets, the body begins to nag at you, "I'm hungry!" That's why you hustle off to the snack wagon when it pulls up outside your workplace. And if you choose high-glycemic snacks, you are setting yourself up for being very hungry at dinnertime. You end up eating too much, and the added weight taxes your heart.

One of the bad results of this vicious cycle is the potential for insulin resistance. For someone who is overweight, the body does not respond to insulin in the normal way. As a result, blood sugar in the system can remain high for long periods, causing the pancreas to produce more insulin. This can result in Type II diabetes, and you do not want to go there.

Not all carbohydrates are good. There may be times when you crave a sugar high, but ideally, you should focus on carbs with a low glycemic index. But contrary to what many people think, not all carbohydrates are bad. There are certain complex carbohydrates with a low glycemic index that provide valuable nutritional elements and should not be eliminated from the diet. Examples of these would include fruits, vegetables, and whole-grain products. So while some of the principles of the low-carb diets are valid, we believe trying to cancel all carbs out of your diet leads to an unbalanced diet and is unwise. We will share more about carbs in chapter 12.

Trend 3: Eat More, Move Less

This trend didn't have its origin in the health community; it is a reflection of American culture and consumerism. It's the widespread trend to eat more than we need and exercise less than we should. This trend is like a double-barreled shotgun aimed right at your heart. It is the primary reason that we are experiencing an epidemic of overweight and obese people in this country.

You can see signs of the "eat more" side of this trend wherever food is found. Think about the all-you-can-eat specials offered at many restaurants and the popularity of buffet-style restaurants. In these situations diners almost feel obligated to go back for seconds and thirds just to get their money's worth. Think about fast-food places where "extra-large" or "super-sized" combos cost only parking-meter change more than regular-sized ones. These tantalizing offers appeal to our sense of value: getting more for less.

In every aisle of the supermarket you are tempted by the "value" of buying sizes of packaged foods larger than what you really need or taking advantage of "buy one, get one free" specials. Almost anyone these days can join one of the popular warehouse chains where you can buy foods—including those you should eat only in moderation—in bulk quantities at even greater savings. The end result of bargain shopping is a full pantry that tempts many families to prepare and serve larger quantities of food at the dinner table.

We are also influenced to eat more than we should through the medium of advertising. For example, in a TV commercial, dinner plates are piled high with pasta. Why? Because if you take the hint and pile your plate just as high, the pasta company will make more money. When we buy more, cook more, serve more, and eat more as advertising often encourages, it means more profit for everyone in the "food chain"—except for the consumer, who must deal with the added calories and pounds.

There's nothing wrong with buying food in volume quantities as long as you still serve it and eat it in healthy portions. Unfortunately, a lot of people are lacking in this discipline. The United States Department of Agriculture (USDA) notes that the average American consumes around 3,500 calories per day, which is roughly twice as much as the normal adult needs to maintain ideal body weight. This is a trend that can kill you. *How much* you eat is at least as important as *what* you eat. In part 3, we will show you how to eat the right foods in the right quantities.

Eating more is especially harmful when it is coupled with the other facet of this trend: moving less. American culture during the past several decades has trended away from a physically active lifestyle to one that is much more sedentary. Thanks to technology, many of us have machines to do the "labor" that a previous generation had to perform by the sweat of their brow. So we move less on the job, with many of us sitting stationary a good portion of the workday. We take the escalator or elevator instead of climbing the stairs. We drive or take the bus when we could walk.

Almost everybody knows it's good to participate in moderate regular exercise as a way to burn up some of the excess calories that most of us consume. Regular exercise provides many other benefits, including stress relief, cardiovascular health, muscle tone, and flexibility. But many of us have trouble carving out time for exercise in our busy lives and maintaining an exercise program that is boring or difficult. In chapter 15, we will share with you exercise options that will help you put together a program that is right for you—and fun!

The damaging "eat more, move less" trend must be reversed. Almost all of us would do well to eat less—as well as smarter—and move more through regular, purposeful exercise.

Trend 4: Eat on the Run

Your son has a dentist appointment right after school, then he goes straight to soccer practice at five o'clock. You drop him off at the field, hurry to pick up your daughter from cheerleading practice, and shuttle her to Brittany's house for pizza with other ninth-grade student council leaders. Picking up

Jason from soccer, you only have a half-hour before you must leave for a parents' meeting at the school. What do you do for dinner tonight? Thank goodness for drive-through windows at places like McDonald's, Wendy's, Taco Bell, Pizza Hut, and KFC.

This scenario reflects another societal trend that can work against heart health. Life for so many of us runs at such a fast pace that meal preparation is more an issue of convenience than nutrition. The combination of our jobs, our other activities, the kids' activities, church activities, classes, sports, and so on leaves little time and energy for planning and preparing nutritious meals. So it is often simpler and easier to stop at a fast-food place en route or to pick up a precooked meal on the fly.

The problem is that convenient eating is not always nutritious eating. The calorie count for a meal in a box or a bag is sometimes off the charts, way more than an adult or a child needs to maintain ideal body weight. The bread products you get are usually refined instead of whole grain. The meats are often high in fat and/or cooked in fat. Fruits and vegetables are seldom an option for these meals. And a fast-food lunch or dinner just doesn't seem to be complete without French fries. To top it off, you can super-size your order or get a combo meal for only a few cents more.

Don't get us wrong; we're not campaigning to close down fast-food restaurants. As you know, many of these establishments offer relatively healthy options, such as salads, low-calorie sub sandwiches, whole-grain breads, and grilled meats. And in reality, an occasional fast-food combo meal or slice of pepperoni pizza dripping with cheese won't kill you. But whenever you need a quick lunch or dinner on the run for yourself and your family, we recommend that you select healthy meals in sensible portions. And we encourage you to balance your occasional fast-food experiences with nutritious, well-balanced, calorie-conscious meals you can prepare at home.

Our approach to heart health in this book is not a new fad diet and exercise plan you will grow tired of in three months. Total Heart Health is an ongoing lifestyle that will help you rise above the temptations that come with the popular trends in food and exercise. Since our approach to health does not eliminate any food groups, you will enjoy a wide variety of options for diet and exercise that won't leave you feeling restricted or punished as so many plans do.

Not only is your physical health at risk due to misconceptions about food and exercise, but your spiritual health may be endangered by myths that can erode your faith and weaken your spiritual heart. Dr. Young will address this vital topic in the next chapter.

Chapter 9: Diet and Exercise Trends
You Don't Want to Follow

- Trying to keep up with some of the popular trends for diet and exercise can be harmful to your health.

- *Trend 1: Forgo All Fats.* A popular health trend has gained wide acceptance suggesting all fats are bad, so we should exclude fat from our diet. This assumption is false because dietary fat in proper amounts is essential for normal body health.

- *Trend 2: Cancel Out Carbs.* Complex carbohydrates with a low glycemic index, like those in fruits, vegetables, and whole-grain products, provide valuable nutritional elements and should not be eliminated from the diet.

- *Trend 3: Eat More, Move Less.* Culture and consumerism tempt us to eat more and exercise less than we should. Almost all of us would do well to eat less, and smarter, and move more through regular, purposeful exercise.

- *Trend 4: Eat on the Run.* Convenient eating is not always nutritious eating. Whenever you need a quick lunch or dinner, select healthy meals in sensible portions. Balance occasional fast-food experiences with nutritious, well-balanced, calorie-conscious meals prepared at home.

- The Total Heart Health plan is not a new fad diet and exercise plan; it's an ongoing lifestyle that will help you rise above the temptations that come with the popular trends in food and exercise.

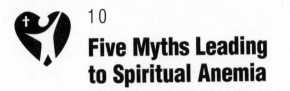

10

Five Myths Leading to Spiritual Anemia

What you mistakenly believe
about spiritual heart health can hurt you.

Dr. Ed Young

Two little boys were playing, pretending to be astronauts. "I think we should land a rocket ship on the sun," said Billy.

Jackie was slightly older and had already studied about the sun. "You can't do that!" he said.

"Why not?" Billy wanted to know.

"Because the sun's surface is about a zillion degrees hot, and we'll get burned up before we get there!"

Billy smiled because he knew he had the solution. "Then we'll go at night."

Fortunately, Billy's childish idea poses no credible threat to the future of space exploration. In fact, isn't it amazing what NASA has accomplished in space since its inception in 1958? Meticulous planning by some of the world's finest scientific minds has resulted in astounding feats being performed at the highest levels of safety for the astronauts. Yes, lives have been lost along the way—*Apollo I, Challenger, Columbia*. But even these tragedies have served to expand knowledge, perfect technology, and improve safety.

There are many fields where what you don't know can hurt you. In some cases, even what you *do* know—when what you know is wrong or inadequate—can hurt you or someone else. Mike and Rick have shared with us how misinformation about fats, carbs, and protein can lead to heart problems. Bad information in the healthcare field can sometimes be fatal. A doctor misdiagnoses an illness, and the patient gets worse or dies. A highly touted wonder drug is recalled and banned when dangerous side effects outweigh its benefits. We have come a long way since a patient's health was thought to be restored by purging, starving, vomiting, and bloodletting. But doctors are, at times, still imperfect in their diagnoses and cures.

What a man doesn't know or mistakenly accepts as true about his spiritual heart can also negatively impact his spiritual health. There are a number of myths in circulation today that are like spiritual placebos. They go down easy and they won't really hurt you, but neither can they do what the right substance can do for you. And if all you take are sugar pills, you will miss the nutrients you need for a strong spiritual heart.

Here are five spiritual heart health myths and what you need to know about them.

Myth 1: Reading Your Bible Means You're Close to Jesus

"Does anyone know what's in the Bible?" a Sunday school teacher asked.

Young Tommy raised his hand. "I know what's in my mom's Bible. Two birthday cards, a Valentine's card, a lot of names written in the front, and a lock of my hair in the back."

Most of us know a lot more about the contents of the Bible than Tommy. Depending on your background in Sunday school and church, you may be able to recite the sixty-six books of the Bible in order—and know that Hezekiah isn't one of them. Like a lot of us who grew up in Sunday school, you may have earned a drawer full of little prizes for memorizing Bible verses and reciting them in front of the teacher. And when the preacher gives a Bible reference in church, you can find it in your Bible faster than anyone in your row because you were a "Bible drill" champ as a kid or youth.

I learned as a boy that when the Bible was being read, something important was happening. When my mother read the Bible aloud, I wasn't allowed to talk or whisper or look away to read something else. My brother and I had to sit as still as possible—no easy feat—as Mother read. If she detected I wasn't concentrating, I would feel her laserlike glare. It was ingrained in me early that, whether I understood it or not, the Bible merited my full attention.

In college, I minored in Bible. In seminary, my professors talked about the Bible almost exclusively. And in all five churches I have served, I have begun my sermons by saying, "Please open your Bible." Each week I've heard the *whoosh* of hundreds of pages being turned, and it is thrilling. And all five of those churches grew dramatically, not because I was a powerful preacher but because the Bible is a powerful book, and something supernatural happens when it's opened and seriously received.

If you came to faith in Christ as an adult, you likely learned early on that the Bible is indispensable to spiritual growth and health. You may have been challenged to read something from the Bible every day—a chapter or a few pages, for example. Many men today, regardless of Bible history, view Bible reading like taking vitamins or medicine. An apple a day keeps the doctor away, and reading the Bible each day keeps the devil away. And somewhere in this emphasis many people begin to assume—or are told by Christians they trust—that the more you read the Bible, the closer you'll be to Christ.

Bible reading is vitally important to spiritual health. But simply knowing the Bible doesn't automatically foster a close relationship with Christ any more than reading *Baseball Weekly* makes you close buddies with Jeff Bagwell or Alex Rodriguez. Many people have memorized huge sections of the Bible but do not have a loving, personal relationship with Christ. There's more to knowing Christ than Bible reading.

Think of knowing Christ personally as a journey and the Bible as your road map. You can't make the journey without the Bible, but if you substitute the road map for the thrills, adventure, and comradeship of living with Jesus, you have wrongly assessed what the Bible is for, and you'll miss out on the great adventure of knowing Christ intimately.

Meriwether Lewis and William Clark began exploring the expansive Louisiana Purchase in 1804. Their prime cheerleader was President Thomas Jefferson, who was eager to see a detailed map all the way out to the Pacific Ocean. Discovery of a Northwest Passage would open America to the trade riches of the East. So with primitive maps in hand, Lewis and Clark and their band set out from St. Louis on May 14.

Imagine one of the grizzled members of the Lewis and Clark party staying behind in St. Louis to read the available maps instead of going into the wilderness with the expedition. He may call himself an explorer, but he didn't blaze any trail and discover new wonders. And most of all, he missed the experience of a lifetime, traveling with America's most famous explorers, Lewis and Clark. He's nothing more than a map reader.

You read the road map of the Bible to know who to follow, where to walk, and how to walk on this expedition we call life. But if you don't get out and walk with Christ, you've missed the point of why God gave us the Bible. A relationship with Jesus means journeying with Him out in the world, doing what He says, and trusting in His help everywhere you go and in all your endeavors. So get into the Bible every day, but don't stay there. Let what you read get out of you as you put it into practice through Christ's presence and power in your life.

Myth 2: Immersing Yourself in Christian Culture Makes You a Better Christian

As Western culture has pulled away from its biblical moorings, the Christian subculture has emerged and flourished. Evangelical Christians have their own radio and TV networks, book publishers, magazines, pop music artists and labels, colleges and universities, retirement communities, and so on. Flip through the yellow pages, and if you want to do business exclusively with Christians, you can patronize merchants displaying an *ichthus*—the sign of the fish—in their ads.

It may be possible to totally immerse yourself in this Christian world, kind of like living in a little heaven on earth. And a lot of Christians think that's how we become stronger Christians. The idea goes that the more time we spend surrounded by Christian people, Christian books, Christian music, Christian entertainment, and so on, the closer we will be to Christ. The flip side of this view would be part of the myth: any time spent outside overt Christian influences—such as attending secular movies, reading secular books, watching network television, and so on—diminishes spiritual vitality and intimate fellowship with Christ.

These assumptions are not categorically true. Don't get me wrong. I appreciate all the good Christian resources at our disposal today, and I thank God for the freedom in our country to use them and enjoy them. But immersing yourself in Christian culture is no substitute for nurturing a relationship with Christ behind the culture. In fact, sometimes, being surrounded by Christian influences can be a deterrent to drawing close to Christ. Instead of getting to know God for ourselves, we rely on our favorite radio teachers, authors, and entertainers to interpret Him for us.

I think it might be more accurate to say that the less we are immersed in the Christian culture, the greater our opportunity to grow as a Christian. Think about it: where is the church the most vibrant and effective at reaching others for Christ? In the Third World regions of Asia, Latin America, and Europe. Many of these places don't enjoy the luxuries of a church on every corner, Christian radio and TV programming 24-7, and abundant copies of the Bible and Christian books and tapes. In some cases, Christians who possess these resources are subject to arrest and even execution. Yet the church is thriving and growing in these areas.

I'm not campaigning against Christian radio, books, magazines, music, and other expressions of the Christian "subculture." We are blessed to have what we have, as long as we don't equate these blessings with intimacy with Christ. The only thing you and Christ need to maintain a dynamic, fruitful relationship is you and Christ. Everything else is gravy. Make use of it, enjoy it, but don't let it distract your focus from Christ Himself.

Myth 3: Praying at Mealtimes Defines Spiritual Leadership

In the old Western classic *Shenandoah*, Jimmy Stewart plays Charlie Anderson, a craggy Civil War–era farmer in Virginia who dotes on his family, treasures his privacy, and tries to isolate himself from the battles around him. His wife is dead, but Charlie still wanders out to her grave and talks to her. She always wanted him to be "religious," so he tips his hat to God by praying at suppertime.

Charlie gathers his big family around the table and offers the same prayer before every meal, something like, "O Lord, we planted the seed, then harvested the crop. If we had not put the food on the table, it wouldn't be sitting here. But Lord, we give You thanks anyway. Amen." By doing so, apparently the old farmer thought he had fulfilled his wife's hopes that he be the spiritual leader of the family.

In my work with men over the years, I can assure you that the "Charlie Anderson myth" is still in circulation. Most of the Christian men I encounter accept the biblical reality that God wants them to demonstrate spiritual leadership where they live and work. But not many of them have a clear idea of what spiritual leadership looks like. The commonly accepted myth is that if you can pray good prayers out loud, such as at mealtimes with others, at bedtimes with wife and kids, anytime a public prayer is called for, then you're really up there in the spiritual leadership department. And if you consistently take the initiative to lead in prayer instead of being nagged into it, well, sainthood can't be too far away.

Let's take this myth into the world of football and see how it sounds. *The quarterback who takes control in the huddle and calls the play with confidence demonstrates team leadership.* Even the casual fan probably won't buy that definition of team leadership. Sure, making the right calls with confidence in the heat of the game is of great value to a team. But that's just a fraction of what it means to be a team leader. Players today talk about guys being leaders in the locker room, on the practice field, and in public as well as during the game. Real leaders work hard all the time. They provide a positive example. They encourage and inspire. They sacrifice for the good of the team.

In a similar way, spiritual leadership goes far beyond "audiblizing" prayers on behalf of others, as worthwhile and admirable as it may be. The focus of true leadership isn't prayers or performance; it's people. As Dr. John Maxwell says, "The first step to leadership is servanthood." Spiritual leadership is all about serving others and meeting their needs. Jesus was the prime example: "The Son of Man . . . came to serve, not be served—and then to give away his life in exchange for the many who are held hostage" (Matthew 20:28 MSG). An unknown writer said, "Blessed is the leader who seeks the best for those he serves."

Demonstrating spiritual leadership in the workplace, in your home, in your church, and anywhere else means accepting responsibility for those around you, serving them, and meeting their needs however you can. It means living the example of a Christian man who is committed to Jesus Christ and His Word at all costs. And it also means praying, not just at mealtimes and bedtimes, but whenever a coworker, family member, friend, or stranger needs the connection with God you can facilitate through your compassion and intercession.

Myth 4: Developing a Pure Heart Means to Quit Sinning

An acquaintance of mine saw this story in the newspaper several years ago. It really happened. Two police officers spotted a young man staggering along the roadside carrying a Bible under one arm. The other arm was tucked tightly under the Bible in an attempt to stem the flow of heavy bleeding where the man had cut off his own hand! The officers retrieved the severed hand from a trashcan, and doctors sewed it back on his arm. The young man said he cut off his hand to obey the words of Jesus in Matthew 5:30: "If your right hand makes you stumble, cut it off and throw it from you."

You may remember a more recent news story of a wilderness hiker in Utah whose hand became trapped when a huge boulder fell on it. He waited five days for someone to find him and free him. But by then he was suffering from dehydration and hypothermia, and his hand was already decomposing from loss of circulation. So, in order to save his own life, he broke the bones in his wrist, cut off his hand, and hiked out.

It's a spine-chilling thought, but I suppose I could do what this hiker did if I had to save my life. But I can't imagine doing what the first young man did: cut off a perfectly good hand just because he couldn't stop shoplifting, stealing money from his roommate, or whatever his hand had done to make him "stumble." The preceding verse sounds just as grisly: "If your right eye makes you stumble, tear it out and throw it from you" (v. 29).

Was Jesus literally telling us to start hacking off any body parts that get us into trouble? If so, our churches would be filled with self-mutilated, blind amputees! No, Jesus had already explained that the source of the evil that we do is the evil attitude of the heart (see vv. 21–28). He was urging us to pursue a pure heart at all costs.

Yet there is this myth among Christian men that the pure heart God desires in us is achieved solely by eradicating sinful thoughts and actions. Don't harbor tempting thoughts. Don't swear. Don't look at another woman lustfully. Don't feed your eyes or your mind pornography. Don't lash out in anger. The litany of sinful behavior is endless.

Using another football analogy, this approach to purifying the heart reminds me of a team that is committed to winning games with defense. They spend most of their free-agent money and draft picks on top-ranked linemen, linebackers, cornerbacks, and safeties. They can smother other offenses with their blitzing rush, tight coverage, and smash-mouth tackling. The problem is, this defensive powerhouse can't win a game because the subpar offense doesn't score many points.

I like the popular gridiron adage "The best defense is a good offense." A good football team needs a good defense. But as long as your offense controls the ball and eats up the clock, the other team can't score.

The same is true in the pursuit of a pure heart. To be sure, you need to exercise discipline over your thoughts, words, and actions. But the best defense is a good offense. You need to pursue purity, not just defend against impurity. How? The instruction King David gives to young men applies to all of us:

> How can a young man keep his way pure?
> By keeping *it* according to Your word.
> With all my heart I have sought You;
> Do not let me wander from Your commandments.
> Your word I have treasured in my heart,
> That I may not sin against You. (Psalm 119:9–11)

Contrary to the myth, developing a pure heart means to saturate it and fortify it against sin with God's pure Word. In yourself, you can't mount a defense strong enough to ward off the assault of the world, the flesh, and the devil against you. But as you "eat up the clock" daily by spending time in God's truth, you automatically begin to build up a strong defense against sin.

Myth 5: Keeping Busy at Church Is How You Accomplish God's Work

The story is told of a young man who was passionately determined to be a firefighter. He signed up with the city's fire department and was immediately shipped off to the firefighters' academy. He excelled in his studies and the practical training, and he graduated at the top of his class.

The young man enjoyed the academy so much, he immediately applied for a position on the faculty and, because of his sterling academic record, was accepted. He began training other recruits and eventually became the most respected instructor on the staff. He moved up to administration and was elected president of the academy. After forty years with the department, he retired with great honors. And during his entire career with the fire department, he never fought one real fire!

Some of us mistakenly believe that the work of the church is synonymous with church work. There's a subtle difference here. By "church work," I mean all the activities and ministries associated with a church's week-to-week, year-to-year schedule. Church work requires church workers to get things done. In our church, for example, we have literally thousands of people involved every week in such roles as teachers, choir members, ushers, greeters, parking attendants, nursery workers, office workers, and so on.

By "the work of the church," I mean our mission as Christians here in this world. It's the same mission Jesus had when He walked this earth. He states it clearly in Matthew 18:11: "The Son of Man has come to save that which was lost." Rick Warren writes, "The mission Jesus had while on earth is now *our* mission because we are the Body of Christ. What he did in His physical body we are to continue as His spiritual body, the church. What is that mission? Introducing people to God!"[1]

Ideally, all our church work is helping to accomplish the work of the church. But, like the skilled firefighter who never fought a fire, we can be so busy at the "academy"—our churches—that we have little time for "fighting fires"—being out on the front line sharing our lives with the lost around us.

For example, your non-Christian neighbor invites you over to shoot pool after work, but you have to say no because you're expected at a church stewardship dinner. He asks about next week, but you've got choir practice on Tuesday night, Bible study on Wednesday night, and a committee meeting on Thursday night. These are all good things, but being so wrapped up in "doing" church may be hindering you from "being" the church in the world, which is God's work for us.

The work of the church is usually accomplished outside the church building, because that's where the lost are. Find your niche of service, whatever it may be, in your local church. But don't forget that Christ is at work outside your church, and He calls you to join Him in His mission to the lost.

Rev. Sam Shoemaker was pastor of Calvary Episcopal Church in New York in the mid-1900s and had a hand in the formation of Alcoholics Anonymous. But his life mission was "the work of the church," reaching the lost for Christ. Here's how he stated it in his poem, "I Stay Near the Door: An Apologia for My Life":

I stay near the door.
I neither go too far in, nor stay too far out,
The door is the most important door in the world—
It is the door through which men walk when they find God.
There's no use my going way inside, and staying there,
When so many are still outside and they, as much as I,
Crave to know where the door is.
And all that so many ever find
Is only the wall where a door ought to be.
They creep along the wall like blind men,
With outstretched, groping hands,
Feeling for a door, knowing there must be a door,
Yet they never find it . . .
So I stay near the door.

The most tremendous thing in the world
Is for men to find that door—the door to God.
The most important thing any man can do

Is to take hold of one of those blind, groping hands,
And put it on the latch—the latch that only clicks
And opens to the man's own touch.
Men die outside that door, as starving beggars die
On cold nights in cruel cities in the dead of winter—
Die for want of what is within their grasp.
They live on the other side of it—live because they have found it.
Nothing else matters compared to helping them find it,
And open it, and walk in, and find Him . . .
So I stay near the door.

Go in, great saints, go all the way in—
Go way down into the cavernous cellars,
And way up into the spacious attics—
It is a vast, roomy house, this house where God is.
Go into the deepest of hidden casements,
Of withdrawal, of silence, of sainthood.
Some must inhabit those inner rooms,
And know the depths and heights of God,
And call outside to the rest of us how wonderful it is.
Sometimes I take a deeper look in,
Sometimes venture in a little farther;
But my place seems closer to the opening . . .
So I stay near the door.

There is another reason why I stay there.
Some people get part way in and become afraid
Lest God and the zeal of His house devour them;
For God is so very great, and asks all of us.
And these people feel a cosmic claustrophobia,
And want to get out. "Let me out!" they cry.
And the people way inside only terrify them more.
Somebody must be by the door to tell them that they are spoiled
For the old life, they have seen too much:

Once taste God and nothing but God will do anymore.
Somebody must be watching for the frightened
Who seek to sneak out just where they came in,
To tell them how much better it is inside.
The people too far inside do not see how near these are
To leaving—preoccupied with the wonder of it all.
Somebody must watch for those who have entered the door,
But would like to run away. So for them, too,
I stay near the door.

I admire the people who go way in.
But I wish they would not forget how it was
Before they got in. Then they would be able to help
The people who have not yet even found the door,
Or the people who want to run away again from God.
You can go in too deeply, and stay in too long,
And forget the people outside the door.
As for me, I shall take my old accustomed place,
Near enough to God to hear Him, and know He is there,
But not so far from men as not to hear them,
And remember they are there, too.
Where? Outside the door—
Thousands of them, millions of them.
But more important for me–
One of them, two of them, ten of them,
Whose hands I am intended to put on the latch.
So I shall stay by the door and wait
For those who seek it.
"I had rather be a door-keeper . . ."
So I stay near the door.[2]

There are other ways the vitality of your spiritual heart can be threatened. In the next chapter, we'll look at several of them.

Chapter 10: Five Myths Leading to Spiritual Anemia

- What a man doesn't know or mistakenly accepts as true about his spiritual heart can negatively impact his spiritual health. There are a number of myths in circulation today that are like spiritual placebos.

- *Myth 1: Reading Your Bible Means You're Close to Jesus.* You can't make the journey of knowing Christ personally without the Bible; but if you substitute the road map for the thrill of living with Jesus, you'll miss the great adventure of knowing Christ intimately.

- *Myth 2: Immersing Yourself in Christian Culture Makes You a Better Christian.* The only thing you need to maintain a dynamic, fruitful relationship with Christ is Christ Himself. Everything else is gravy. Enjoy them, but don't let them distract your focus from Christ.

- *Myth 3: Praying at Mealtimes Defines Spiritual Leadership.* As with a football quarterback, spiritual leadership goes far beyond "audiblizing" prayers. The focus of true leadership isn't prayers or performance, but people.

- *Myth 4: Developing a Pure Heart Means to Quit Sinning.* The best defense is a good offense. Pursue purity by developing a pure heart through saturating and fortifying it against sin with God's Word.

- *Myth 5: Keeping Busy at Church Is How You Accomplish God's Work.* Ideally, our church work (serving in church) helps us accomplish the work of the church (reaching people for Christ). Our church work is done inside the church, but the work of the church is done outside, in the world.

11
Spiritual Heart Problems Just Waiting to Happen

Is anything gumming up your heart? Clean it out now.

Dr. Ed Young

Everybody in town knew Anthony, and Anthony was everybody's friend. This husband and father of three young kids was outgoing, witty, and animated in everything he did. He was a respected small-business owner and a driving force behind his community's Little League program. And he was a lay minister in the five-hundred-member church his family attended. Being Mr. Personality, Anthony spearheaded the church's assimilation ministry, making sure new attendees received a personal call or visit, organizing and teaching the new members' classes, and helping people find their niche of service in the church.

Then one evening, Anthony disappeared. He left the house for a meeting at church and never came home. Later that night, Nina called a pastor who was at the meeting, but he said Anthony never showed up. He didn't come home that night or the next or the next. No note, no phone call about where he had gone. Nina eventually discovered that some of his clothes, his shaving kit, and a gym bag were missing. Then she found out that a large portion of the couple's savings had been withdrawn from the bank the day before Anthony left. There were no signs of foul play. All the evidence suggested that Anthony had just run away, leaving his distraught family to pick up the pieces of their shattered lives.

It was years before a few shreds of information came together to tell the story. Anthony had apparently been living an invisible second life. Nina discovered to her horror that Anthony's other life involved homosexuality, male prostitution, and organized crime. She couldn't accept that he was a whole-hearted participant, believing rather that he had been seduced and coerced until he was trapped in the darkness. Anthony never came home.

Anthony had a hidden heart problem. Many people talk about heart problems. Some are referring to the physical heart—valves not functioning properly, clogged arteries, arrhythmia. Others are talking about pain in the emotional heart, describing wounds resulting from discord in a friendship, romance, or family relationship. But the most serious heart problems occur in the spiritual heart, because the spiritual heart is at the core of our being. It appears that Anthony had an untreated spiritual heart problem that eventually plunged him into serious trouble.

Spiritual heart problems were Jesus's topic when He said, "Do you not understand that everything that goes into the mouth passes into the stomach, and is eliminated? But the things that proceed out of the mouth come from the heart, and those defile the man. For out of the heart come evil thoughts, murders, adulteries, fornication, thefts, false witness, slanders. These are the things which defile the man" (Matthew 15:17–20).

Blockages in the spiritual heart are serious, and serious damage will occur if the problems are not rooted out and dealt with.

In Need of a Spiritual EKG

One morning, a friend of mine noticed a new smell in his house. It was the faint odor of decaying flesh. He searched every room but could not find the source. Day after day the odor intensified, and he became desperate to find the problem. At last he found the source. A doorknob had punched a little round hole in one of the bedroom walls. Apparently a small bird had flown into the house and found its way inside the bedroom wall through that hole. The bird became trapped and died. My friend was so desperate to remove the stench of death from his house that he was willing to tear out the drywall to remove the bird carcass.

In a similar way, when there is blockage in the spiritual heart, we don't feel right or live right. It's like a foul odor we can't put our finger on. We must do whatever is necessary to find the source and get rid of it, or things will only get worse. This must have been David's determination when he prayed, "Investigate my life, O God, find out everything about me; cross-examine and test me, get a clear picture of what I'm about; see for yourself whether I've done anything wrong—then guide me on the road to eternal life" (Psalm 139:23–24 MSG).

David understood that any corruption in his life originated in his heart. From that sick center, infirmity spread over his whole being like the reek of death that seeped through my friend's house. A blockage in the spiritual heart can shut down the flow of spiritual energy and passion for the Lord. David recognized that only God can get to the source of a clogged heart. Only He has the power to rip out the deadness of sin concealed in the hidden depths of our hearts.

How do these debilitating blockages form? Just as plaque builds up in the coronary arteries to block the flow of blood to the physical heart, so our spiritual hearts are blocked when foreign matter enters to compromise their purity. Second Kings 17:33 says that God's people "feared the LORD" but "served their own gods." Jesus said, "If a kingdom is divided against itself, that kingdom cannot stand" (Mark 3:24). The apostle James wrote that a "double-minded man, unstable in all his ways," cannot expect to receive anything from the Lord (James 1:8). "Unstable" literally means this person cannot walk a straight line when it comes to faith and ethics. That seems to have been Anthony's problem. A divided, compromised heart is weak because the flow of the Spirit's energy to that person's life is blocked.

At times you may feel distant from God and disconnected from what you know He wants you to be and do. In this state, it's easy to beat yourself up mentally, thinking you're no good to God and worthy of only His anger and punishment. Maybe you've been ragging on yourself for some time, hoping that the guilt and shame you feel will somehow fix what's wrong.

But by now you may have discovered that condemning yourself this way brings no relief. That's because it was never intended to. Jesus said in Matthew 5:8, "You're blessed when you get your inside world—your mind and heart—put right. Then you can see God in the outside world" (MSG). The opposite of a blocked heart is a pure heart. God is not out to hammer you about having a clogged heart; He wants to make you pure in heart by removing whatever is blocking your fellowship with Him. You will never fully understand and enjoy the blessing and assurance of God unless you allow Him to purify your heart.

Undergoing Spiritual Angioplasty

What do these debilitating spiritual blockages look like? Let's consider five ways the spiritual heart can be blocked and how to return to a pure heart in each case.

The Buildup of Sin

Wrongs against God and others that are not confessed and forgiven are the biggest and most threatening blockage to a pure heart. Like the tiny particles of plaque that collect in the arteries, the clog of unconfessed sin usually begins very small in the spiritual heart but grows into a major blockage. Eventually it can cut off the "blood supply" to your life, which is the flow of God's energy through His Spirit.

How does it happen? Usually in small, subtle ways that compound into large, unavoidable problems. Yet God could not have made it any easier for us to remove these paralyzing blockages. The Bible says, "If we admit our sins—make a clean breast of them—[God] won't let us down; he'll be true to himself. He'll forgive our sins and purge us of all wrongdoing" (1 John 1:9 MSG).

Confessing sin means to say the same thing about it that God does. We may start out by rationalizing, "It's not so bad"; but God says, "It's wrong; it's sin." We say, "Everybody else is doing it"; but God says, "It's wrong; it's sin." We say, "It will all balance out in the end"; but God says, "It's wrong; it's sin." Only when we say what God says—"It's wrong; it's sin"—can He say, "Exactly right. You're forgiven, the blockage is removed, and your heart is pure again."

The sooner you follow the Great Physician's prescription for dealing with the heart blockage of sin, the sooner you will again enjoy God's life coursing through your heart.

The Buildup of Anger

Have you ever wished your car was armed with fender-mounted rockets when a reckless driver cuts you off?

When you're in a hurry to get something fixed but discover you bought the wrong part, are you tempted to punch a fist through a wall?

Have you ever been upset with a coworker whose incompetence makes your work harder and causes you to look bad?

Have you simmered in anger over a child who repeatedly fails to follow through with his or her chores?

Do you occasionally get mad at your wife or a good friend who seems to want more of your time and attention than you are able to give?

Every man alive gets angry at times. It's a normal human emotion that signals an area of life that needs our attention. But unresolved anger builds an obstruction to spiritual vitality. It leads to bitterness. The Bible tells us that the root of bitterness, when it grows up, defiles many (see Hebrews 12:15). So the spiritual heart disease of unresolved anger and bitterness is contagious. Normally we don't think of heart disease as being contagious, but it can be hereditary, passed down through a family. This is how anger and bitterness can affect "many."

The Greek language used in the Bible has two words for "anger." One brings to mind a flame burning a small clump of dry straw. It flares up and then fades. The other word describes sustained anger, as if the person continually adds more straw to keep the blaze alive and hot. This is brooding anger, anger you refuse to release, anger that seeks revenge. Jesus says that this kind of anger is the equivalent of murder (see Matthew 5:21–22). Anger clogs the heart of love, forgiveness, and compassion, essential components of Christ's character in us.

The Bible has the prescription for keeping anger from blocking the flow of your spiritual heart: "Go ahead and be angry. You do well to be angry—but don't use your anger as fuel for revenge. And don't stay angry. Don't go to bed angry. Don't give the Devil that kind of foothold in your life" (Ephesians 4:26–27 MSG).

Reader's Digest version: *Deal with it!* Don't soak in your anger. Pray it out, talk it out, and work it out if necessary with the object of your anger. If you don't, you're simply inviting the devil to clog up your heart and make your life worse.

The Buildup of Addictions

Life is often difficult and painful because we are sinful people who live in a world of sinful people. We sometimes get cheated, betrayed, slighted, or attacked—and these things hurt the heart. Whenever we experience physical pain, we seek medicines from the doctor that will cure the ailment and end the pain. But when we are hurt emotionally and spiritually, we usually end up medicating ourselves in ways that temporarily numb the pain but rarely cure the malady. These self-administered "drugs" often become addictions that block the flow of God's life to our hearts.

Self-medicating can take many different forms, but the goal of all of them is to mask the pain with momentary relief or pleasure. So we go for anything that makes us feel good for a time. These "drugs" can range from actual drugs—tobacco, alcohol, marijuana, cocaine, painkillers, or sleeping pills—to more socially acceptable substances like caffeine, food in general, and more harmful foods in particular. Sometimes the medication is sex when a man turns to pornography or seeks an illicit physical or emotional connection to soothe the pain in a troubled relationship. There are also the emotional and spiritual drugs of pop psychology, cults, psychics, and unscriptural religious experiences. As with any drug, repeated use leads to addiction; we can't function without that substance or experience.

The apostle Peter wrote, "So be content with who you are, and don't put on airs. God's strong hand is on you; he'll promote you at the right time. Live carefree before God; he is most careful with you" (1 Peter 5:6–7 MSG). Picture anxiety as being pulled in different directions at the same time. That sounds like real life, doesn't it? But instead of handling anxiety with self-prescribed cures that will accumulate in a blockage in the heart (both spiritually *and* physically in some cases), God invites you to give your anxiety to Him and let Him deal with it. Why? Because He cares for you and wants to save you from the additional pain your cares and supposed cures will cause.

The Buildup of Spiritual Indifference

Neglect and indifference toward the Lord, His kingdom, and His Word clog the spiritual heart. This is a slow-moving process, so subtle it may not be noticed until the heart is cold toward God. You become lax at prayer, Bible study, church attendance, and fellowship with supportive Christian friends. At first, there may be a pang of guilt. Denial eases the guilt, and the heart hardens a bit. This is followed by apathy. You just don't care about spiritual things anymore. Church is boring, and the Bible no longer makes any sense because the blockage of indifference robs your heart of understanding.

Paul wrote, "[Christ] was supreme in the beginning and—leading the resurrection parade—he is supreme in the end. From beginning to end he's there, towering far above everything, everyone" (Colossians 1:18 MSG). The antidote to the blockage of spiritual indifference is to consciously and purposefully give Christ first place in every area of your life.

The Buildup of Idolatry

Idolatry is a major obstruction to spiritual vitality. Idolatry simply means you're serving the wrong god. How do you know if you are following the wrong god? Ask yourself two key questions.

What do I fear above all else? There may be an idol attached to your fears. For example, it's natural to fear the loss of a loved one, such as a parent, a wife, or a child. But an unnatural fear in this area may signal that you are placing that loved one above God. And anything that can be placed in a casket should not be the object of our worship.

What do I think about most when I don't have to think about anything else? When you've finished work for the day and are alone with your thoughts, what fills your mind? Do you rush to the television? A computer game? An Internet chat room or a tantalizing Web site? Be careful: an idol may be tucked in there somewhere, especially if those thoughts are an obsession you can't shake!

Paul wrote in 2 Corinthians 3:18, "We all, with unveiled face, beholding as in a mirror the glory of the Lord, are being transformed into the same image from glory to glory, just as from the Lord, the Spirit." Galatians 5 describes the image into which a Christian man is being transformed if his spiritual heart is increasingly free of idolatry: "love, joy, peace, patience, kindness, goodness, faithfulness, gentleness, self-control" (vv. 22–23). As you focus on filling your heart with the characteristics of Christ, the blockages in your heart will be dissolved.

When you become a Christian, you are launched into a process we call spiritual growth. Just as everything about you is coded in a tiny strand of your DNA, so your complete maturity in Christ is in your "spiritual DNA." You just need to grow into what God has already determined you to be in response to your faith in Him. Blockages in the spiritual heart need to be removed because they impede your growth and transformation. This means you can be a Christian and not be growing, thereby missing the joy of what God has for you in this life.

But as we continue to look at Christ, His nature and character are like a laser that penetrates the heart and melts the blockages. The more we focus on Jesus and His glory, the greater is the flow of spiritual transformation and power in our lives, allowing us to become like Him!

We have talked about the unique valor of a man's heart and the enemies that threaten to rob you of this valor. In part 3, we provide you with positive strategies for keeping your heart strong so you can be a blessing to God, to your family and friends, and to the world God calls you to serve. Drs. Duncan and Leachman begin by teaching you about the proper fuels you need for a healthy physical heart.

Keys to Total Heart Health

Chapter 11: Spiritual Heart Problems
Just Waiting to Happen

- Just as plaque builds up in the coronary arteries to block the flow of blood to the physical heart, so the spiritual heart is blocked when foreign matter enters to compromise its purity. A divided, compromised heart is weak because the flow of the Spirit's energy is blocked.

- *Buildup of Sin.* Wrongs against God and others that are not confessed and forgiven are the most threatening blockages to a pure heart. Only when we say what God says—"It's wrong; it's sin"—can the blockages be removed.

- *Buildup of Anger.* Don't soak in your anger. Pray it out, talk it out, and if necessary work it out with the object of your anger.

- *Buildup of Addictions.* Instead of handling anxiety with self-prescribed cures that will accumulate into a blockage in the heart, God invites you to give them to Him and let Him deal with them.

- *Buildup of Spiritual Indifference.* Neglect and indifference toward the Lord, His kingdom, and His Word clog the spiritual heart. The antidote is to consciously and purposefully give Christ first place in every area of your life.

- *Buildup of Idolatry.* Two questions help you discern if you're following the wrong god: What do I fear above all else? What do I think about most when I don't have time to think about anything else? As you focus on filling your heart with Christ's characteristics, idolatry is displaced.

Part 3

The Foundation Stones for
Strengthening a Man's Heart

12
Fueling Up for a Stronger Heart

Eating right will help you ripple in places
where you now jiggle.

Dr. Michael Duncan and Dr. Richard Leachman

Energy balance is vital for a healthy physical heart. As mentioned earlier, your "energy in"—the daily calories you take in through food—should be about the same as your "energy out"—the calories you expend in daily activity. When the balance between the two is roughly even, your weight stays about the same. More energy in than energy out, and you gain weight—and run the risk of the attendant health problems. More energy out than energy in, and you lose weight. Energy balance is one of the foundations of Total Heart Health.

In this chapter and the next, we will talk about the energy-in side of the equation: a healthy diet. In order to encourage physical heart health, you need to pay attention to the kind of fuel you put into your body. In chapter 15 we will explore the energy-out side: exercise. Our recommendations on both sides will help you achieve the energy balance you desire to reach your physical health goals.

Fuel for Your Body

Your eyes widen as the waiter sets before you the dinner you've been waiting for: a side of baby back ribs, a mountain of cole slaw, and a man-sized hunk of garlic toast. We don't mean to spoil your appetite, but what you're really looking at are the different metabolic fuels your body will use to keep you alive and functioning for the next several hours. Enjoying a delicious meal, especially in a setting of conversation with other people around a table, is one of life's more pleasant experiences. But long after you've left the restaurant, your gastrointestinal system will be breaking down and sorting through that meal in search of the energy your heart must deliver to every cell in your body to keep you alive and well.

The key to the fuels you put into your body is getting the quality and quantity you need for optimum health. Too much of the wrong kinds of food—and sometimes even too much of the right kinds—and your body suffers. You won't feel as well as you could, you may not like how you look, and you run the risk of serious, life-shortening disease.

When we talk about fuels, we're talking about the three basic metabolic fuels contained in the wide variety of things we eat. Everything you eat gets broken down into three nutritional elements: fats, carbohydrates, and proteins. In a nutshell, the magnificent digestive system God created in you transforms these three fuels into the energy you need.

Since calorie count is integral to energy balance, it is important to note the number of calories in each of the three metabolic fuels. Each gram of carbohydrates contains four calories. Protein also contains about four calories per gram. Fat, however, is more energy-dense, containing nine calories per gram. This makes fat a very efficient metabolic fuel; you can go a long way on a small amount. Unfortunately for most of us, fat is *too* efficient. We usually take in more dietary fat than we burn, which means the excess goes to storage—body fat.

Carbohydrates	1 gram = 4 calories
Protein	1 gram = 4 calories
Fat	1 gram = 9 calories

Alcohol is another energy-dense, calorie-rich food substance that weight-loss candidates sometimes overlook. Every gram of alcohol contains about seven calories. So even a glass of wine with dinner or the occasional bottle of beer piles additional calories onto the foods we eat. Furthermore, since alcohol is frequently an appetite stimulant, you may end up eating more food when alcohol is consumed with the meal. And, of course, for those people who drink more, caloric input increases proportionately.

Facts About Fats

The fat in the food we eat is made up of chains of molecules called fatty acids. There are four major types of fatty acids, but they are not all created equal when it comes to a healthy diet. It is important to know the differences between them and how these differences can affect your energy balance. We often differentiate between the fatty acids by calling them "bad" fat—which includes saturated fatty acids and trans fatty acids—and "good" fat—which includes monounsaturated fatty acids and polyunsaturated fatty acids.

"Bad" Fat

Saturated fatty acids are found primarily in animal fats, which is why we urge moderation—but not total abstinence—when it comes to eating red meat and dairy products such as whole milk, ice cream, butter, and cheese. Other sources of saturated fat are tropical oils such as palm oil, coconut oil, and cocoa butter.

Saturated fatty acids are a significant threat to Total Heart Health. A little bit goes a long way, and a lot can do serious damage. Saturated fat increases blood cholesterol and triglycerides, the two major fats circulating in the blood. The American Heart Association recommends that fewer than 7 percent of your total daily calories come from saturated fat.

Fish, chicken, olive oil, and canola oil are low in saturated fats, and you can chalk up zero saturated fat for nonfat dairy products, fruits, vegetables, beans, bread, and rice. The difference can be rather profound in a daily diet. Notice the comparisons of saturated-fat content below:

3.5 ounces of hamburger	8 grams
3 ounces of baked salmon	1 gram
1 tablespoon of butter	12 grams
1 tablespoon of canola oil	1 gram
1 cup of whole milk	5 grams
1 cup of nonfat milk	0 grams

3.5 ounces of fried chicken	5 grams
3.5 ounces of skinless baked chicken	2 grams
1 small slice of cheesecake	9 grams
1 large peach	0 grams

Trans fatty acids are the real black sheep of the dietary fat family. They are artificial fatty acids, made by hydrogenating or partially hydrogenating polyunsaturated fatty acids. You will find trans fat in processed and packaged foods requiring fat because it is more stable than polyunsaturated fat, meaning these foods don't spoil as quickly. If a packaged product contains hydrogenated or partially hydrogenated vegetable oil, then it contains trans fat. "Hydrogenated" or "partially hydrogenated" and "trans fat" mean the same thing.

Trans fatty acids seem to be a staple in junk food: packaged cookies, cakes, doughnuts, crackers, pastries, microwave popcorn, white bread, margarine, and deep-fried foods. For example, one doughnut has 3.2 grams of trans fatty acids, and a large order of fries has 6.8 grams. Foods with zero trans fat include unprocessed vegetables, fruits, grains, nuts, vegetable oils, legumes, and soy milk.

There are a lot of tempting, tasty comfort foods on the trans fat list. But beware: trans fatty acids can be trouble. There are some major adverse health problems associated with trans fatty acids. The net negative effect of trans fat on your system is about double that of saturated fat. For example, trans fat hits you with a one-two punch in the cholesterol department. Trans fatty acids have been found to increase bad cholesterol (LDL) and decrease good cholesterol (HDL).

The preservative value of trans fat is overshadowed by its punishing effect on the heart. According to the *New England Journal of Medicine,* if you replace just 2 percent of your energy intake from trans fatty acids with monounsaturated or polyunsaturated fatty acids, you decrease the risk of coronary heart disease by a whopping 53 percent.[1]

"Good" Fat

Monounsaturated fatty acids are one of two "good" fats. Most of the monounsaturated fatty acids are found in plants. Some prime sources are olive oil, canola oil, safflower oil, and avocados. Whenever you can replace saturated fat with monounsaturated fat, you lower your bad cholesterol without lowering your good cholesterol.

Another good fat, polyunsaturated fatty acids, is found in plant products such as sunflower oil, corn oil, flaxseed oil, pumpkin oil, walnut oil, and soybean oil and in cold-water fish such as Chinook salmon, albacore tuna, anchovy, herring, mackerel, and Pacific halibut. Polyunsaturated fatty acids are essential to ongoing good health. Since the body does not manufacture them, we must include in our diet foods that have them.

Omega-6 and omega-3 are polyunsaturated fatty acids with great benefits to heart health. Omega-6 is found in animal meat, milk, eggs, vegetable oils, seeds, and nuts. Most of us do pretty well getting omega-6 because its sources are common menu items in most homes. Omega-3 is found in leafy green vegetables, flax, flaxseed oil, canola oil, walnuts, Brazil nuts, fish, and fish oil.

Medical research is discovering some wonderful heart benefits from omega-3, and eating fish significantly factors into the results. A study of twenty-two thousand men over a seventeen-year span revealed remarkable positive results from omega-3. Men with the highest level of omega-3 in their blood were 80 percent less likely to experience sudden death.[2] In an Italian study of eleven thousand male heart-attack survivors, those assigned to take fish oil supplements daily were 53 percent less likely to die suddenly than those assigned to take a placebo.[3] And omega-3 works just as well for women. One study tracked eighty-five thousand women over a sixteen-year period. Those who ate fish at least once a week experienced a 30 percent lower risk of heart disease. And women who ate fish at least five times a week lowered their risk by 45 percent.[4]

So when it comes to dietary fat, don't overlook the polyunsaturated varieties, especially omega-3. Plan cold-water fish into your weekly diet. The payoff will be a decreased risk of sudden cardiac death, arrhythmia, elevated blood triglyceride levels, and blood clots.

Total Heart Health Recommendations for Fats

When it comes to fat, our recommendations for Total Heart Health will be fairly obvious to most people, but here they are:

Decrease saturated fat. We're not suggesting that you completely give up steaks and other red meats. But instead of ordering a Texas-sized Porterhouse when you go out, select a six-ounce cut of lean beef or fish instead. If you treat yourself to a burger, get one with a single patty instead of two or three. When buying ground beef at the market, select packages with a lower fat content. Also cut back on dairy products or go with low-fat or nonfat varieties.

Greatly decrease trans fat. Ideally, we would be better off to eliminate consumption of trans fat. But it would be difficult for most of us, because trans fat is in so many of the packaged food products we buy at the market. Careful monitoring is the key. It won't kill you to have an occasional Oreo or two, but if you can't stop with one or two, don't bring them into the house. The same goes for other packaged baked goods. Also, cut way back on fried foods. For example, grill or broil your chicken and fish instead of frying it in a skillet or deep-frying it. Relegate French fries to a rare treat in your diet instead of a weekly staple.

Replace saturated fat and trans fat with monounsaturated and polyunsaturated fats. Instead of using spreads like butter or margarine, try dipping your bread in olive oil and herbs as we do in Italian restaurants. Include vegetable oils, nuts, flaxseed, and flaxseed oil in your diet. And most important of all, eat fish, such as cold-water salmon (not farm-raised) and water-packed albacore tuna (not oil-packed). You may even consider fish oil supplements to maximize the benefits of omega-3.

Clues About Carbs

Another major metabolic fuel is carbohydrates. Starches are the major carbohydrates in most diets: bread, beans, rice, pasta, potatoes, corn, and so on. Carbohydrates are essentially sugars. There are three basic types of carbohydrates in a normal diet: starches, which are the major type; sucrose, which is table sugar; and lactose, which is the main sugar found in milk products. During the digestive process, starch, sucrose, and lactose are broken down into the elemental sugar molecules of fructose, glucose, and galactose, which are absorbed into the bloodstream and burned as energy.

Glucose is vitally important to all metabolism. It is the universal fuel for all human cells. Your muscles need glucose for physical activity, which is why athletes need high levels of carbohydrates in their training diet. The brain and red blood cells rely heavily on glucose as a primary fuel source. The brain can at times operate on other types of fuels, but your red blood cells are 100 percent dependent on glucose for their function.

Carbohydrates are generally grouped under two headings—simple and complex.

Simple Carbohydrates

Simple carbohydrates can be easily broken down and absorbed in the intestinal tract to provide energy in a hurry. You want simple carbs when your blood sugar is plummeting and you need a quick energy boost. Examples of simple carbs are fruit juices, soft drinks, and refined foods such as white bread, white rice (especially the instant variety), potatoes, and certain types of crackers and cereals.

Simple carbs deliver needed calories quickly, but they provide little else in the way of nutrients the body needs. That's why the calories from simple carbs are often referred to as "empty calories." And that's why you are more likely to be hungry sooner after eating simple carbs than after eating complex carbs.

We use sweeteners of various types to make food taste better, and most of these sweeteners are simple carbohydrates—sugars. There are two kinds of sweeteners: nutritive and non-nutritive. Nutritive means it has caloric value and little else—empty calories. Some examples are table sugar, honey, fructose, and brown sugar—which is nothing more than table sugar flavored with molasses. Non-nutritive sweeteners are most commonly found in those little pink, blue, and yellow packets many people use at mealtimes in place of sugar. These powdery sugar substitutes, which are up to seven hundred times sweeter than table sugar, are made from amino acids, aspartic acid, and phenylalanine. Non-nutritive sweeteners are an acceptable option for adding a sweet taste without adding calories. But stay informed about the possible disadvantages of non-nutritive sweeteners.

Complex Carbohydrates

We also need complex carbohydrates, which provide calories while also supplying nutritional elements such as vitamins, minerals, fat, fiber, protein, phytochemicals, and antioxidants. Complex carbs are found in foods such as whole-grain breads, oatmeal, peas, lentils, beans, whole fruits (instead of juices), and brown rice (instead of white rice). Complex carbs take longer to process in the digestive system, but they provide more of the nutrients we need and help forestall feelings of hunger.

Any glucose in your system you don't use up in activity and exercise is stored in limited amounts in the liver and muscle in a complex called glycogen. Once those storage facilities are full, additional glucose is packaged into fat particles and transported to adipose tissue in the body for storage. So the key is to limit carbohydrate intake so that only a minimal amount is stored as fat.

Total Heart Health Recommendations for Carbohydrates

Our Total Heart Health recommendations will again seem rather obvious once this basic information is understood.

Decrease intake of simple carbohydrates. Cut back on table sugar and honey on cereal, in coffee and tea, and in other uses. Non-nutritive sweeteners are an alternative to consider, but ask your doctor first about the potential negative effects in the sweeteners you use. If you're a meat-and-potatoes kind of guy, reduce your portions of potatoes and/or substitute other vegetables. And draw a decisive line in the sand when it comes to sweets like cookies, cakes, and sugary soft drinks, rationing out to yourself only a modest amount.

Increase intake of complex carbohydrates. Eat plenty of fresh vegetables and fruits. When you eat breads and cereals, make sure they are the whole-grain variety. And include adequate amounts of fiber, healthy fats, and protein in your daily diet.

Points About Protein

Protein is the third major metabolic fuel. Unlike fat and the glucose from carbohydrates, your body cannot store amino acids. So you need amino acids and protein in your diet every day. A healthy diet requires about one gram of protein per kilogram (2.2 pounds) of body weight—and we're talking about your ideal weight according to the body mass index. Men generally require about sixty-five grams of protein per day, while women need about fifty grams. Most of us equate protein with meat. But there are other very good sources of protein you can work into your diet that won't elevate your saturated fat intake as meat does. Here are several examples, compared to the protein in meat:

Meat, poultry, fish	4 ounces cooked (90 grams)	28 grams protein
Milk or yogurt	1 cup	8 grams protein
Egg	1 medium	7 grams protein
Cheese	2 slices (60 grams)	14 grams protein
Legumes	1 cup	7 grams protein
Peanut butter	2 tablespoons	14 grams protein

There is a definite weight-control benefit of increased protein in the diet. The stomach empties slower with protein due to the prolonged digestion process. As a result, nutrient absorption is slowed and you will feel full longer, meaning you may not be as tempted to snack between meals. But remember: If you rely heavily on red meat for your protein needs, you will be loading up on saturated fat, which negates the weight-loss benefit.

When it comes to sources of dietary protein, there are two types: *complete* protein and *incomplete* protein.

Complete Protein

Foods with complete protein contain all the essential amino acids, and foods with incomplete protein lack some essential amino acids. Generally speaking, animal protein is complete protein, so a reasonable amount of meat and eggs in your diet is okay. A lot of men equate protein with red meat, which is loaded with saturated fat and cholesterol. But there are other sources of protein. Fish is an excellent source of protein as well as omega-3 fatty acid, so you are doing your body a lot of good when you eat fish.

Incomplete Protein

Plant protein tends to be incomplete protein because most foods from plants are missing some essential amino acids. Sources of plant protein include whole grains, nuts, beans, and other legumes. Soy has been a hot diet topic in the last few years because it is the only plant that is a complete protein. In addition to all the amino acids, soy offers a number of health benefits. Fortified soy products are an excellent source of vitamins B$_{12}$ and D, and soy may lower bad cholesterol. But there may be some adverse neurological effects connected to soy, so we recommend using soy products in moderation.

Total Heart Health Recommendations for Protein

Our Total Heart Health recommendations for protein intake include the following:

Increase plant sources of protein. Take advantage of protein sources such as beans, nuts, and whole grains.

Eat more fish. Fish, especially the cold-water variety, is doubly beneficial. It is an excellent source of protein and it supplies valuable omega-3 fatty acids.

Moderate the intake of beef and dairy products. Smaller portions of lean beef are better for most people than giving up meat altogether. And when you include dairy products, go for low-fat or nonfat varieties.

Avoid high-protein diets. In chapter 17, we will discuss many of the diet fads on the scene today and highlight their strengths and weaknesses. But the bottom line for most of them, including high protein, is that a balanced approach to nutrition is better.

In the next chapter, we will continue this discussion of dietary fuels by exploring items such as cholesterol, fiber, vitamins, and minerals.

Chapter 12: Fueling Up for a Stronger Heart

- Everything you eat gets broken down into three nutritional elements: fats, carbohydrates, and proteins. It's important to note the number of calories in each of the three metabolic fuels.

- "Bad" fat is saturated fatty acids found primarily in animal fats, which is why we urge moderation in eating red meat and dairy products. Trans fats, artificial fatty acids, are the real black sheep of the dietary fat family, found in many processed and packaged foods.

- Monounsaturated fatty acids, found mostly in plants, are "good" fats. Another "good" fat is polyunsaturated fatty acids, found not only in plants, but also in cold-water fish.

- We recommend you decrease your consumption of saturated fat, greatly decrease trans fat, and replace saturated fat and trans fat with monounsaturated and polyunsaturated.

- Carbohydrates are simple or complex. Simple carbs deliver needed calories quickly but provide little nutrition. Complex carbs take longer to digest but provide more nutrients.

- We recommend you decrease your intake of simple carbohydrates and increase your intake of complex carbohydrates.

- Proteins are categorized as complete and incomplete. Complete protein foods—like meat and eggs—have all essential amino acids. Incomplete protein foods—like plant foods—lack some of the essential amino acids.

- We recommend you increase your intake of plant sources of protein, eat more fish, moderate your intake of beef and dairy products, and avoid high-protein diets.

13

Fuel Additives That Can Increase Performance

Cholesterol, fiber, vitamins, minerals—and what they mean in your daily diet.

Dr. Michael Duncan and Dr. Richard Leachman

Fats, proteins, and carbohydrates are the major components of the metabolic fuels you need for daily energy. But there are a lot of other dietary health terms floating around that you may be wondering about. Let's talk about several of them and learn how they can help or hinder heart health.

Cholesterol and Triglycerides: Traveling Companions

Cholesterol and triglycerides are the two major fats circulating in the bloodstream. Cholesterol is not strictly a nutritional issue, but it is an important health issue that is often talked about with fat, so let's look at it more closely.

Cholesterol

Cholesterol is a fat, and most of the cholesterol in your body is manufactured by your liver. The cholesterol in the food you eat does not necessarily translate one-to-one to the amount of cholesterol circulating in your bloodstream. But you do want to monitor your cholesterol intake and do what you can to keep your blood cholesterol within healthy limits.

We have already learned about the two types of cholesterol. LDL is "bad" cholesterol, and HDL is "good" cholesterol. Few people can remember which is which, so you might think of them by their first letters: LDL can make your life *lousy,* and HDL can make your life *happy.* LDL in the bloodstream accumulates on the walls of the arteries as plaque, which can, over time, result in blood clots, blockage in the arteries, and possibly a heart attack. HDL in the bloodstream actually carries away some of the LDL particles and has been known to cause a reduction in plaque buildup or atherosclerosis.

So HDL and LDL are kind of like the cops and robbers of the circulatory system. When LDL is rampant, you've got big trouble brewing. As we learned when talking about fats, trans fatty acids in your diet can induce a cholesterol "crime spree" in your bloodstream, increasing LDL while decreasing HDL. But when HDL is on the job in force, it can greatly reduce cholesterol "crime" in your arteries. So it is important to do whatever you can to decrease LDL while increasing HDL.

It is now recommended that your total cholesterol be no greater than 200 mg/dl. As for LDL, if you have fewer than two risk factors (diabetes, smoking, hypertension, family history, low HDL), your bad cholesterol should be no higher than 160 mg/dl. If you have two or more risk factors, your LDL should be no greater than 130 mg/dl. And if you have been diagnosed with coronary artery disease, your LDL should be kept at 70 or less.

As for HDL, we mentioned earlier that men tend to have lower levels of HDL than women do. So an HDL value of 35 mg/dl is normal for men, while 45 mg/dl is the normal range for women.

There are two known ways to beef up the "police force" of HDL in your bloodstream. The first is regular exercise. The second, which is still under some debate, is alcohol. Some doctors and nutritionists today recommend one to two drinks three to five days per week. Consult your doctor or nutritionist for the latest data on this topic as well as for treatment options.

Triglycerides

Triglyceride is the other major fat in your bloodstream. Elevated triglyceride levels can contribute to development of coronary artery disease, but high levels are a less-potent predictor of CAD than cholesterol. Persons with excessively high triglyceride levels are at risk of developing pancreatitis—severe inflammation of the pancreas.

Elevated triglycerides have also been associated with the metabolic syndrome, which comprises a group of metabolic risks found in an individual. A person with metabolic syndrome characteristically suffers from all of the following: central obesity, or excessive fat tissue around the midsection; high triglycerides and low HDL, contributing to plaque buildup in the arteries; insulin resistance or glucose intolerance; diabetes; and elevated blood pressure. This syndrome predisposes the patient to cardiovascular disease.

Elevated triglycerides are dramatically corrected by reducing the intake of carbohydrates and sugars. While there are certain genetic aberrations that can lead to elevated triglycerides, the overwhelming majority of these patients are obese and/or suffer from diabetes. Once again, poor diet and eating habits are at the root of the problem, and changing those habits and embracing a Total Heart Health lifestyle can help reverse them.

Dietary Fiber: Making the Most of Your Meals

Dietary fiber is a plant substance that is virtually indigestible. In other words, the fiber you get in the foods you eat travels entirely through your intestinal tract without being absorbed into the system as fats, carbohydrates, and proteins are. Most fiber is a complex carbohydrate that the body cannot break down.

There are two classifications of fiber: soluble and insoluble. Both are necessary to digestion and health.

Soluble Fiber

Soluble fiber is found in foods that contain ingredients such as oat bran, pectin, psyllium, legumes, guar gum, mucilages, and citrucell. If the last two words look familiar, it's probably because you have seen fiber supplements in the drug aisle of your supermarket with similar brand names: Metamucil and Citrucel. In a normal diet, you gain the benefits of soluble fiber from such foods as oatmeal, barley, beans, lentils, apples, pears, bananas, citrus fruits, and Brussels sprouts.

The soluble fiber in your food forms a gel in the stomach and small intestine as digestion begins. This gel expands in the stomach and slows emptying, allowing you to feel full longer, which may help you cut down on between-meal snacks. The gel continues to move slowly through the small intestine, allowing for slower absorption of nutrients and bile salts from your food. And since digestion is moving in slow motion, carbs are not as rapidly broken down and absorbed, which keeps your glycemic index in a healthier range.

As the mass moves through the large intestine or colon, it undergoes further fermentation by bacteria, which extracts elements useful to the body's immune system and for fighting cancer, particularly in the colon.

Insoluble Fiber

Insoluble fiber is found in foods containing wheat bran, sterculia, mignin, and methyl cellulose. You get your insoluble fiber from eating whole-wheat products: wheat oat, corn bran, flaxseed, vegetables such as green beans and cauliflower, and the skins of fruit and root vegetables such as potatoes.

The effect of insoluble fiber is focused less on the stomach and small intestine and more on the colon in the digestive process. It helps slow transit time and increases water absorption in the stool. Insoluble fiber also performs what some have called a mop-and-sponge effect by cleaning up potential toxins left over in the intestinal tract.

Fiber is thought to protect against colon cancer, and it is useful in treating constipation, diverticular disease, irritable bowel syndrome, and hemorrhoids. We recommend twenty to thirty grams of dietary fiber per day. The average American diet contains only about fifteen grams, so most of us fall short. The best way to remedy this shortfall is to add more fruits, vegetables, and whole-grain products to your daily menu. You can up your fiber intake, for example, by eating whole-grain breads. A slice of refined-wheat bread has about one gram of fiber, but a slice of whole-grain bread has two to four grams.

Try adding fiber at breakfast. Start with a bowl of whole-grain cereal. For example, a small packet of instant oatmeal gives you about four grams of fiber. You can find other whole-grain cereals with up to ten grams per serving. And don't overlook the fiber advantage in beans—pinto beans, kidney beans, lima beans, navy beans, or black beans—which are high in dietary fiber. You may also want to take a fiber supplement to make sure you're getting enough.

Vitamins and Minerals:
Make Sure You're Firing on All Cylinders

Vitamins and minerals are the essential micronutrients for heart health. There are about forty of them we must purposely take in through the food we eat or through vitamin supplements, because the body cannot manufacture these elements. The four categories are water-soluble vitamins, fat-soluble vitamins, major minerals, and trace minerals.

Water-Soluble Vitamins

Water-soluble vitamins are all the B vitamins as well as vitamin C, also known as ascorbic acid. They are listed below, along with how much of each we need daily. You need far less of the vitamins measured in micrograms (mcg) than those measured in milligrams (mg).

	100% US RDA
B Vitamins	
Thiamine (vitamin B_1)	1.5 mg
Riboflavin (vitamin B_2)	1.7 mg
Pyridoxine (vitamin B_6)	2.0 mg
Niacin (vitamin B_3)	20 mg
Folic acid (folate)	400 mcg
Pantothenic acid	10 mg
Cobalamine (vitamin B_{12})	6 mg
Biotin	300 mcg
Vitamin C (ascorbic acid)	60 mg

They are called water soluble because they are found in the watery portion of food. You need thiamine, riboflavin, niacin, pantothenic acid, and biotin to free energy from your food into your bloodstream. Pyridoxine, cobalamine, and folic acid help metabolize protein and amino acids and are useful in the synthesis of collagen, which is the support structure of the body.

Vitamin C is an antioxidant that is necessary for collagen synthesis, providing skin tone. Vitamin C does not prevent the common cold, but it prevents scurvy and is thought to reduce risk of cancer of the mouth, esophagus, stomach, and breast. Good sources of vitamin C are citrus fruits, bell peppers, spinach, tomatoes, and broccoli.

Folate is necessary for new cell creation. Natural sources include fortified grains, cereals, okra, spinach, orange and tomato juices, turnip greens, and broccoli.

Vitamin B_{12} has been shown to decrease levels of homocysteine, a compound associated with heart disease. Deficiency of vitamin B_{12} can lead to anemia, some neurological diseases, heart disease, and cancer. Good sources include meat, fish, poultry, fortified cereals, eggs, and soy milk.

Generally speaking, it is difficult to get too much of the water-soluble vitamins because the kidneys will flush out what you cannot use. So it's no problem if you forget and take your B and C vitamins twice in the same day. Pyridoxine is the exception and could result in nerve damage. But it is rare for someone to accidentally overdose on it.

Fat-Soluble Vitamins

Here are the fat-soluble vitamins and their daily allowances. We recommend that most people aim for the higher range of vitamin D because many people are deficient in that vitamin. Notice that three of the four vitamins are measured in international units (IU), while vitamin K is measured in micrograms (mcg).

	100% US RDA
Vitamin D	400–600 IU
Vitamin E	30 IU or 15 mg
Vitamin A	5,000 IU or 700 mg
Vitamin K	120 mcg men
	90 mcg women

The fat-soluble vitamins, which come as fatty acids or oils, are absorbed into the lymphatic system, where they are stored in fat or in the liver until your body needs them. Since your body can store them up, there is potential for toxicity with overdoses of these vitamins, so you want to stay close to the recommended daily dosage.

Vitamin A is important for good vision, bone growth, and healthy skin. Sources include beef (especially liver), eggs, and cheese. Beta carotene can also be converted to vitamin A. You get beta carotene in carrots, sweet potatoes, pumpkins, squash, and turnip greens.

Vitamin D is important for calcium and phosphorus metabolism and for healthy bone structure and teeth. You can get vitamin D through salmon, eggs, and fortified foods such as milk and cereals. Vitamin D is also increased through the skin's exposure to ultraviolet-B radiation from sunlight. Adequate levels of vitamin D reduce the risk of colon cancer. Deficiency results in osteoporosis, osteomalacia, rickets, and musculoskeletal pain. The best way to ensure that you are getting at least 400 IU daily is through a vitamin D supplement.

Vitamin E is an antioxidant that may help decrease the risk of Alzheimer's disease when it is combined with vitamin C. But contrary to what some beauty products promise, vitamin E does not prevent wrinkles. Natural sources include vegetable oils, whole grains, nuts, and leafy green vegetables.

Vitamin K is essential for blood clotting. People on blood thinners need to be careful about taking a vitamin K supplement because it may interfere with the anticoagulation properties of the drug. Natural sources of vitamin K include green vegetables, cabbage, milk, and eggs.

Major Minerals and Trace Minerals

The major minerals needed for daily health are sodium, potassium, chloride, calcium, phosphorus, magnesium, and sulfur. Sodium, potassium, and chloride are very important for maintaining proper water and electrolyte balance in your body. Calcium, phosphorus, and magnesium are vital to a healthy bone structure. And sulfur is needed to stabilize protein structure.

We have all been cautioned about the amount of dietary sodium—salt—in our diet. The average American consumes about 4,000 milligrams of salt daily. Government guidelines used to recommend up to 2,400 milligrams daily, but the recommendation has recently been dropped to 1,500. There seems to be an abundance of sodium in most of the foods we eat, so it's a good idea to look for ways to cut back on our use of salt.

Trace minerals, as you might guess from the term, are found in very small quantities in the body. Some of the more common ones are chromium, copper, fluoride, iodine, iron, manganese, selenium, and zinc. Check the label on your bottle of multivitamins for a number of others. But these minerals are absolutely essential for a variety of tasks. Iodine, for example, is used in the thyroid gland to make thyroid hormones. Iron is used to make your red blood cells. Manganese and other trace minerals are used as cofactors in enzyme reactions.

Some men are diligent about planning what they eat to meet their daily vitamin and mineral needs. But we find that most men are just too busy to assure that they are eating a completely nutritional diet. We believe the cost-to-benefit ratio of taking daily supplements of vitamins and minerals just makes good sense. These days you can buy dietary supplements that are made specifically for men and targeted to your age group. As always, check with your doctor to make sure your selection of supplements is right for you.

Water: How Much Is Enough?

It seems everywhere you, go you see people sipping from plastic bottles of water. From the gym to the workplace to the car to the refrigerator in the average home, water bottles abound. The brand name on the label and the style of plastic bottle people prefer are almost fashion statements these days. Many people started buying water at the supermarket in case lots simply because "everybody else is doing it."

This is one popular trend in our culture that is very good for us. Water is an essential nutrient for optimum cell function in the body. Without sufficient quantities of water, the body suffers from dehydration. Fortunately, the kidneys are quite efficient at regulating large variations in water consumption without allowing disease states.

As a general rule, you need one milliliter of water per day for each calorie of energy you expend. In other words, multiply your calorie-need profile by 0.001 to find your daily water need in liters. For example, if you are a moderately active man burning 2,800 calories a day in your activity, you should be drinking about 2.8 liters of water a day (2,800 x 0.001).[1] That roughly translates to about eight twelve-ounce glasses of water. And if you are very active, such as playing sports or working out aggressively, you may want to up your intake to make sure you are properly hydrated for good heart health.

Your heart's health and your body's energy depend on the quality and quantity of fuels you take into your body. The same can be said about the health and vitality of your spiritual heart. Dr. Young will now help you understand how to maximize spiritual heart health through the energy provided by spiritual "fuels."

Keys to Total Heart Health

Chapter 13: Fuel Additives
That Can Increase Performance

- Cholesterol and triglycerides are the two major fats circulating in the bloodstream.

- HDL—"good" cholesterol—and LDL—"bad" cholesterol—are the cops and robbers of the circulatory system. When LDL is rampant, HDL is on the job to reduce cholesterol "crime" in your arteries, so do all possible to decrease LDL and increase HDL.

- Elevated triglyceride levels can contribute to development of coronary artery disease and pancreatitis. Triglycerides are dramatically corrected by reducing intake of carbohydrates.

- Both soluble fiber—which helps you feel full longer—and insoluble fiber—which cleans potential toxins from the intestinal tract—are essential to digestion and health.

- Water-soluble vitamins are all the B vitamins as well as vitamin C. Fat-soluble vitamins include D, E, A, and K.

- The major minerals needed for daily health are sodium, potassium, chloride, calcium, phosphorus, magnesium, and sulfur.

- As a general rule, you need one milliliter of water per day for each calorie of energy you expend. Multiply your calorie-need profile by 0.001 to find your daily water need in liters.

14
Running in the Fast Lane

Are you getting enough high-octane fuel
to stay in the race?

Dr. Ed Young

The 1999 Indianapolis 500 had one of the more unusual finishes in the history of the big race. Skipping his final pit stop, driver Robby Gordon took the lead in the two-hundred-lap race with only thirty-two laps to go. Gordon flew around the track at nearly 200 mph, ticking off the final laps. All he had to do was keep up the pace, and he would get the checkered flag.

But on lap 198, Gordon's engine began to sputter. The powerful racecar slowed, allowing his nearest competitor, Kenny Brack, to narrow the gap between the two front runners. Then on lap 199, the engine in Gordon's car shut down completely, and Brack raced past him to take the checkered flag. With only one lap to victory, Robby had run out of fuel. He coasted into the pits, added a quick shot of fuel, and finished fourth.

"We knew what it was going to take to win this race," Gordon said. "It just slipped away."

The decision to gamble on the final pit stop came from team owner John Menard. "We knew it was close," he said. "But it's the Indy 500, and you've got to go for it. I'm sorry for Robby. We ran him out of fuel. I just feel like crying."[1]

Can you imagine how Robby Gordon must have felt? The finish line was in sight, but he just didn't have the juice to get there. I've never driven a racecar, but I know about feeling empty and ill-equipped for finishing my tasks strongly. Just as Menard and Gordon discovered, if you want to run strong and finish well in this race of life, you better keep your spiritual tank full of high-octane fuel.

High Octane for High Performance

Just a glimpse at the life of Jesus reveals that He expended tremendous energy day by day in His ministry of teaching and healing. For example, when Jesus was touched by the woman with the hemorrhage, He felt power leaving Him (see Mark 5:25–34). Imagine the power drained from Jesus's body every day as He ministered to the needy crowds who thronged around Him. Yes, He was God, but He was God wrapped in human flesh. He got hungry and weary just as we do. Where did He get the energy to meet the great spiritual demand on Him?

The Gospels record that Jesus prepared for His ministry with prayer, often rising long before sunrise to seek out a secluded spot to commune with His Father. We also learn that it was His custom to be in the synagogue on the Sabbath to worship and read from the Old Testament scrolls (see Luke 4:16). If Jesus needed "energy in" to nurture His spiritual heart and equip Him for the "energy out" of ministry, how much more do we?

Being a pastor, I know what it feels like to be spiritually drained. At the end of a long Sunday of ministry, you can knock on me and hear nothing but an echo because I feel so empty. Your situation may not be quite the same, but you know what it means to sense the spiritual and emotional energy being sucked from you as the day goes by. It may be the stress of working at a job with a grouchy boss and whining coworkers. It may be a stressful home situation, conflicts in the neighborhood, demanding relatives, or needy friends.

The key to energy balance for Jesus was knowing how to replenish His energy. Jesus purposely energized Himself in the Father's presence, and as He did so, He was more than a match for the demands of His ministry. I want to share with you several essential principles for spiritual energy balance. It all starts with "energy in," receiving from God the fuel you need to nurture a strong spiritual heart.

Fill 'er Up

I have learned the value of starting each day with prayer. My first routine upon rising is to kneel beside the bed and pray. Often I use an acrostic to help me stay on track as I pray: the letters SELF. These four letters remind me how important it is to bring my*self* to God as the day begins. If it is difficult for you to focus your thoughts first thing in the morning, I recommend this simple outline to you. It need only take a moment or two. Here's how it works.

S is for *surrender*. Paul urged believers to present their bodies to God as a living and holy sacrifice (see Romans 12:1), so I offer myself to God in complete surrender at the beginning of the day. I ask for and yield to His agenda above my own. I encourage you to do the same. Surrender doesn't mean you become invisible. Rather, by surrendering to God, you put yourself at His disposal to become His highly visible and useful instrument in the world.

E is for *empty*. Jesus said, "Self-sacrifice is the way, my way, to finding yourself, your true self" (Matthew 16:25 MSG). Self-sacrifice means emptying myself of anything that could interrupt the flow of God's energy into my life. This is the time in my prayer when I confess my sin, weakness, and inadequacy and receive God's forgiveness according to 1 John 1:9.

L is for *lift*. Next, I spend a few moments lifting my praise and worship to God. Worship in the Bible is often associated with the physical posture of lifting up to God. The Psalms urge us to lift up our voices, our heads, our hearts, and our hands to God in worship and adoration. As you lift yourself up to God, you are in perfect position to receive the outpouring of the energy you need.

F is for *fill*. Ephesians 5:18 commands us, "Be filled with the Spirit." Having surrendered to God's agenda, emptied myself of every hindrance, and lifted my heart to God in worship, I ask the Holy Spirit to fill my life completely. This is what it means to tap into God's energy supply.

And notice the promising results of this infilling: "Speaking to one another in psalms and hymns and spiritual songs, singing and making melody with your heart to the Lord [instead of harping, criticizing, and blaming]; always giving thanks for all things [instead of whining, grousing, and complaining] in the name of our Lord Jesus Christ to God, even the Father" (vv. 19–20). Will your day be more productive and fruitful as you draw on the energy of the Spirit? Count on it!

The Word of God is another essential element for filling your spiritual tank. You may not have time for a lengthy Bible study every morning, but at least spend a few moments in the Word, such as reading and meditating on a few verses, listening to a devotional on tape or on the radio, or memorizing or reciting Bible passages as you drive to work.

Run Your Own Race

Jesus recognized everyone's importance. On His way to the home of a synagogue official to heal his desperately ill daughter, Jesus was touched by a woman who needed healing from a persistent hemorrhage. In that culture, women were treated as inferior, and perhaps this woman was only a lowly peasant. In contrast to the synagogue official's needs, her needs may have been judged by the throng to be unworthy of the Master's attention. Yet Jesus interrupted His journey to minister to this woman, even addressing her as "Daughter" (Mark 5:34).

You may be underpaid at work, underappreciated at home, or undervalued in other circles. But take strength in the fact that you are more important to God than you can imagine. In fact, God is looking for people just like you, people who are open to His energy. Second Chronicles 16:9 says, "For the eyes of the LORD move to and fro throughout the earth that He may strongly support those whose heart is completely His."

Go on the Offensive

When it comes to dealing with obstacles and stresses in your life, prayer is your God-given "weapon of mass destruction." Paul writes in Ephesians 6:12, "Our struggle is not against flesh and blood, but against the rulers, against the powers, against the world forces of this darkness, against the spiritual forces of wickedness in the heavenly places." Prayer is how you get through the skirmishes, conflicts, and battles of daily life. John Piper writes, "Until we know that life is war, we won't know what prayer is for."[2] When you pray, you bring God's power to bear on the spiritual forces set against you and against God's purposes in your life.

Sometimes we try to fight the battle with the wrong weapons. We assume we can change things by human tactics, ranging from a sharp corrective word to a violent physical outburst. Trying to win spiritual battles through human means doesn't work. Spiritual conflicts are fought in the spiritual realm, and it takes energized prayer to wage such a battle.

You need to take seriously your role as a pray-er. Throughout the day, be in constant prayer for your wife, your children, your boss, your coworkers, your friends, and even your adversaries. Approach every opportunity, conversation, and conflict with prayer. Pray as you drive, work, play, and work on chores. Spend several moments each day bowed in focused prayer, then sustain that conversation with God even through the busiest moments with quick sentence prayers while you're on the go. Consider implementing different types of fasting; the practice of prayer and fasting is a biblical pattern. When you pray, you are a conduit for God's energy to meet the needs around you.

Don't Overlook the Little Things

We men seem to be created for big things. We have this drive to conquer our challenges, accomplish great feats, and expand our influence. I don't know about you, but I am highly energized for the big stuff in my life. I'm motivated to pray long, work hard, and bite the bullet to accomplish my goals.

Then I get home and have to take out the garbage or clean out the garage or pay the bills or . . . you get the picture. Life isn't all about the big, exciting stuff that gains us the satisfaction, attention, and material rewards we enjoy. It's also about the little stuff—chores and responsibilities we don't enjoy very much but have to do. I find that the mundane duties of the day drain me instead of energize me. Can you relate?

When we get bogged down and sucked dry by the little things, 1 Corinthians 10:31 should be our motivation: "Do everything . . . heartily and freely to God's glory" (MSG). Everything—that means *everything*, including the stuff we don't get paid for or recognized for. When we devote these tasks to God as an act of worship, just as we often do the more important tasks, the energy we need from Him to follow through is always there.

Sure, the taxes still need to be figured out and the gutters cleaned out, but what if you dedicated these tasks to the glory of God and did them to please Him? It will make a tremendous difference in both your motivation and your energy level! So whatever you must do—take the trash barrels to the street, write boring reports, clean out the attic, change diapers—do it for Him. You will experience the satisfaction of knowing your effort is bringing glory to God.

Keep Your Eye on the Road

Pursuing God's energy doesn't mean you must be a recluse. Strike a balance between your times of quiet solitude and busy service to others, between activities of private inspiration and social engagement. Some Christians become so heavenly minded they are of little earthly good. Rather than walking in a spiritually energized relationship with God and the people around them, they retreat into a kind of Christian mysticism. "Worldly" responsibilities such as caring for family and earning a living are viewed as bothersome interruptions to such "heavenly" pursuits as Bible conferences, church meetings, and personal studies.

Yes, you need to spend time nurturing your body, soul, and spirit. But if you use "spirituality" as an excuse to marginalize or ignore others, you are misusing the energy God has placed at your disposal. God doesn't fill you with His Spirit just so you can be spiritually fat and happy; He pours His energy into you to empower you for service. Move toward a good balance between personal nurturing and ministering to the needs of others.

Be a Role Model

Those of us who enjoy watching sports hear a lot about athletes being role models. Some accept the role willingly and strive in at least their public lives to be positive examples for their fans, especially kids. Other athletes seem so addicted to the pleasures they can gain through their wealth and fame that they don't care what kind of example they set. In a 1993 Nike TV ad, outspoken NBA star Charles Barkley said, "I am not a role model; parents should be role models."

Like it or not, unless you live your life in a cave all by yourself, you are a role model to someone. The only thing to be decided is what kind of life you are modeling. You may argue, "I'm nothing special; my influence doesn't count for much." Don't sell yourself short. You are a man in whom the Spirit of God resides. As you are energized by Him and then release that energy in service to others, you make an impact. You may not see it right away because the changes in others often happen gradually. But rest assured that your commitment to spiritual heart health will both inspire and motivate others around you to grow in their relationships with God.

You have just as many opportunities to be a conductor of God's energy for influencing others as any other man. Your wife, your children, your friends, your coworkers, your clients, your neighbors—they all need what you have. Tap into the spiritual energy God provides and allow Him to duplicate His work in you in the lives of others you touch day by day.

Now we will talk about the energy-out side of energy balance for your physical heart, which focuses on consistent exercise. Our heart specialists have asked a fitness expert to supply this important chapter on exercise. As Kristy Brown talks about fitness in the next chapter, you'll want to zero in on her expert advice.

Chapter 14: Running in the Fast Lane

- Jesus expended tremendous energy daily, and the key to His energy balance was in knowing how to replenish His energy.

- To get "energy in," it's important to begin each day with prayer. I like to pray using the acrostic SELF:

    S is for surrender to God.

    E is for getting emptied of sin.

    L is for lifting up our voices, heads, hearts, and hands to the Lord in worship.

    F is for being filled with the Holy Spirit.

- The Word of God is another essential element for filling your spiritual tank. Spend a few moments each morning reading and meditating on Bible verses, listening to a devotional tape, or memorizing and reciting Bible passages as you drive to work.

- Throughout the day, be in constant prayer for your wife, children, boss, coworkers, friends, and even your adversaries.

- Strike a balance between quiet solitude and service to others, between private inspiration and social engagement.

- As you are energized by God and then release that energy in service to others, you make an impact. Your commitment to spiritual heart health will both inspire and motivate others around you to grow in their relationships with God.

15
Exercising Your Way
to a Healthy Heart

Sorry, but playing racquetball on Saturday isn't enough to keep you healthy.

Kristy Brown

It seems that everybody has an opinion about exercise. Some are thought-provoking, while others are just amusing. Here are several examples found at various sites on the Internet:

- If it weren't for the fact that the TV set and the refrigerator are so far apart, some of us wouldn't get any exercise at all (comedian Joey Adams).
- Lack of activity destroys the good condition of every human being, while movement and methodical physical exercise save it and preserve it (Plato).
- Exercise is bunk. If you are healthy, you don't need it. If you are sick, you should not take it (U.S. automobile industrialist Henry Ford).
- I take my only exercise acting as pallbearer at the funerals of my friends who exercise regularly (Mark Twain).
- We can now prove that large numbers of Americans are dying from sitting on their behinds (physician and author Dr. Bruce B. Dan).
- *Exercise* is a dirty word. Every time I hear it, I wash my mouth out with chocolate (author unknown).
- The only exercise some people get is jumping to conclusions, running down their friends, sidestepping responsibility, and pushing their luck! (author unknown).
- My idea of exercise is a good brisk sit (comedienne Phyllis Diller).

No matter which "authority" you side with, here is reality: the health of your heart depends on consistent physical exercise. This is the energy-out side of the Total Heart Health equation. Calorie output through physical activity helps offset calorie input through eating to provide the energy balance we need.

Consistency is the key to exercise, as Dan discovered. Dan wasn't one for traditional exercise, but he led an extremely active life. A lawyer in his early forties, Dan worked hard and loved to stay busy in his off time. He took the kids fly-fishing, camping, or hiking about once a month. They also played football in the yard or basketball in the driveway most weekends. And Dan even coached his daughter's soccer team one season. He was very active for a man who spent most of the week in his office.

So when Dan collapsed with a mild heart attack one New Year's Eve, he was as surprised as his family members. His doctor made it perfectly clear that exercise would officially be a regular and permanent part of his life from here on out. After his recovery, he hired a trainer at the fitness center near his office. He signed up to work out twice a week, doing a mixture of cardio exercises and weights. Dan knew twice a week wasn't perfect, but he had a busy law practice and was back to most of his activities with his kids. There was only so much time he could devote to working out. In reality, Dan didn't always make both of his workouts each week. When his court schedule got hectic, he'd have to cancel, but he always made it at least once a week.

After several months, Dan's trainer told him that he wasn't making much progress in his strength training. Dan wondered how that was possible, since he was almost always sore after his workouts. A year after he started exercising, Dan went back for a cardiovascular checkup. The doctor found a small improvement in Dan's cholesterol level, but the blockages in his blood vessels had worsened slightly. Dan was shocked! How was this possible, with all his hard work?

Dan illustrates the "weekend warrior" approach we often see in men with regard to exercise. After five or six relatively sedentary days at the office, most guys think they can get the exercise they need by working strenuously in the yard one day or shooting hoops with the kids or with friends for an afternoon. When your workouts are inconsistent like this, your body never really adjusts to them. Your muscles get really sore, your joints are prone to greater injury, and your strength doesn't improve significantly. And if you're exercising for heart health, the benefits of inconsistent exercise are negligible, as Dan discovered. A consistent exercise program is critical to a healthy heart.

A Biblical Mandate for a Healthy Body

You may ask, "If exercise is so important to physical heart health, why doesn't the Bible say something about it?" Well, the Bible does give us a general guideline for exercise in 1 Corinthians 6:19–20. We come back to this passage often when we talk about anything that can harm physical bodies and thus diminish or shorten our effectiveness to live for Christ in the world. Paul writes, "Didn't you realize that your body is a sacred place, the place of the Holy Spirit? Don't you see that you can't live however you please, squandering what God paid such a high price for? The physical part of you is not some piece of property belonging to the spiritual part of you. God owns the whole works. So let people see God in and through your body" (MSG).

The Bible doesn't specifically prohibit smoking or using harmful drugs. But we know these behaviors can seriously threaten our physical health and even kill us, so we stay away from them in our commitment to glorify God in His "temple"—our bodies. The same goes for eating too much, eating the wrong foods, or failing to get the exercise we need for proper health. Anything we do that endangers the body is disrespectful to God's temple and should be avoided.

But there's another very practical reason that the Bible doesn't specifically command us to participate in physical exercise. Most of those to whom the Bible was originally written didn't have a problem with fitness, because their lifestyle kept them fit. In biblical times, walking was the primary means of transportation. Furthermore, in a predominantly agrarian society, manual labor—farming, herding sheep, and the like—kept people physically active. They had few of the step-saving devices we enjoy today, so everyone logged plenty of steps every day.

Think about Jesus, for example. He was probably in excellent physical condition because He was even more active than most of His contemporaries. Growing up in a carpenter's home, He likely worked with Joseph into adulthood, which required chopping, sawing, and shaping wood. Once His ministry began, He spent three to four years crisscrossing the land of Palestine and beyond on foot, eager to preach, teach, and heal. He traveled between Judea in the south and Galilee in the north countless times, a journey of approximately eighty miles each way. His lifestyle kept Him fit.

Not so with twenty-first-century Americans. Most of us can get through the day without much movement at all. A car takes us everywhere we want to go. We ride the elevator instead of climbing the stairs, take our food off a supermarket shelf instead of growing and harvesting it or hunting for it, and cook by twisting dials on a range or pushing buttons on a microwave instead of gathering wood and building a fire. Many of us work by sitting at a computer all day, and much of the toil of manual labor has been eased by machinery. Unlike people in Jesus's day, most of us have to schedule our exercise outside of our work to keep ourselves fit.

Three Facets of Complete Exercise

A complete exercise program consists of three categories of activity: cardiovascular, resistance, and flexibility. For the best results, combine all three based on your fitness needs. Cardiovascular exercises, the most important, are essential for keeping your heart strong and healthy. Resistance exercises help you with daily activities by developing strength for strenuous tasks such as lifting the five-gallon water bottle into the dispenser, picking up and throwing the kids or grandkids while playing in the pool, or opening the tight lid on a new jar of pickles. Flexibility exercises will keep you mobile and limber with good range of motion throughout life. Let's look at each in detail.

Cardiovascular Exercise for a Stronger Heart

Cardio exercise happens when you move your large muscle groups rhythmically and repetitively, such as in walking, running, biking, swimming laps, dancing, or stairstepping. Sustained, repetitive exercise elevates your heart rate, which facilitates blood flow, delivers oxygen to your cells, and increases metabolic rate.

Even sex is good cardiovascular exercise. Experts estimate that sexual activity can be a significant calorie burner, though you should not assume that a normal, healthy sex life can replace other cardio exercises. And there is considerable evidence that people who exercise consistently have more energy and feel better about their appearance, which typically results in a healthier sex life. Cardio exercise and healthy sex are mutually beneficial.

Cardio exercise is always about progression—starting at a safe, comfortable level and periodically working up to realize greater benefits. Use the FITT scale to guide you as you progress in cardio exercise. *F* is for *frequency*, how many days a week you exercise. *I* is for *intensity*, the speed or energy level you put into your exercise. *T* means the *type* of exercise you do—walking, jogging, stepping, and so on. And *T* is for the amount of *time* you exercise each day. For example, you may power walk (type) at a steady, moderate pace (intensity) five times a week (frequency) for thirty minutes a day (time).

In order to progress, increase your exercise by one FITT component at a time. For example, if you swim laps three mornings a week for forty-five minutes, consider lengthening your swim by five minutes every couple of weeks or adding a fourth morning. If you jog five days a week, you might try increasing the time from thirty minutes to forty minutes.

Always begin your cardio exercise with a four- to five-minute warmup and end with a three- to four-minute cool-down. For example, if you run, warm up with some stretching and walking, and then end your jog by slowing your gait and walking. Warmup allows the heart rate to increase gradually, and cool-down brings it back to normal gradually, which is kinder to your heart.

Resistance Exercise for Muscle Tone and Strength

Resistance exercises—also called strength training or weight training—use force on the muscles to strengthen them. Common resistance exercises are weightlifting, working out on resistance machines, and pressing against your own weight as in push-ups, pull-ups, and sit-ups. The American College of Sports Medicine recommends working all the major muscle groups. You have four primary muscle groups in your legs: gluteals, quadriceps, hamstrings, and calves. Your midsection contains two groups: abdominals and lower back. Exercises in this area are very important to good posture because these groups support your trunk and spine. There are five primary muscle groups in your upper body: pectorals, upper back, shoulders, biceps, and triceps.

We recommend that you work each muscle group with one to three sets of eight to twelve repetitions—or reps—each. For example, eight consecutive push-ups or bench presses translate to one set of eight reps working the chest and triceps. After resting from this set, do another set of eight reps. Your goal should be to gradually increase your reps from eight to twelve and your sets from one or two to three. Develop other exercises to work the other muscle groups, such as squats for your legs and sit-ups for your midsection.

The level of difficulty for your resistance program can be measured on a continuum, moving from challenge to fatigue to failure. Start with a challenge and move to the point of fatigue. When you start out lifting weights, for example, select a weight that feels challenging. When a set of twelve lifts no longer fatigues you, it's time to add more weight. As your fitness level improves, you will be able to push yourself further before becoming fatigued. Over time, keep adding weights until, at the end of a set, you feel like you can't do one more lift—which is fatigue. Those who are more advanced push themselves past fatigue to the point of failure, meaning they keep lifting until they cannot physically complete a lift without the help of a trainer or spotter.

Flexibility Exercise for Range of Motion

Flexibility, which is achieved primarily through stretching, is the most commonly neglected component of exercise. Many people ignore stretching because it doesn't seem to burn calories. But when you stretch properly, muscle fibers get longer. At age twenty, that may not seem like a big deal. But later in life, range of motion becomes crucial. People begin to notice their body tightening at about age forty. Aching backs, for example, can often be alleviated with a few minutes of stretching each day. So no matter what your age, include stretching in your exercise plan to stay limber.

The American College of Sports Medicine recommends stretching all major muscle groups one to three times per workout session, one to three sessions a week. The best way to stretch is to extend the muscle and hold it there for ten to thirty seconds. You should feel tension but not pain. In reality, stretching can be the most relaxing part of your workout.

Some people stretch in the morning; others stretch before going to bed.

Stretching is especially beneficial after a workout. Whenever you stretch, bear in mind that your muscles don't start on "ready." They need to be extended gently and stretched out gradually, especially when the muscles are not warmed up prior to a stretch.

Shaping Up Your Workout Routine

People usually exercise for one or two good reasons: to improve general health and/or to lose weight. No matter what your aim, our Total Heart Health recommendation is that at a minimum, you exercise for thirty minutes a day, five days per week. If you can't start at that level, at least make it your goal. Remember: if you are starting an exercise program for the first time, it is important to talk to your doctor first.

If general health is your goal, you can vary your exercise during the week. The minimum cardio exercise for general health is twenty minutes a day, three days a week. For example, you can walk for twenty minutes a day on Monday, Wednesday, and Friday, followed by ten minutes of core training (exercises for the abdominals and lower back) and stretching. Alternate this routine on Tuesday and Thursday with thirty minutes of resistance training.

In order to build more muscle, exercise a little more than thirty minutes a day, maintaining the three-day cardio and flexibility program while adding ten to fifteen minutes of resistance exercise before or after your cardio. On your two non-cardio days, do extended resistance exercises. To achieve muscle growth (hypertrophy), increase your weights and stay on the lower end of repetitions (eight to ten). Hypertrophy requires that you challenge the muscles. If you're not fatigued after the exercise and sore the next day or so, you should increase the intensity.

In order to lose weight, you must, of course, burn more calories than you take in with food. A minimum five-day, thirty-minute cardio exercise will help you burn calories. Initially you may do twenty to twenty-five minutes of daily cardio activity followed by five to ten minutes of stretching. But move up to a full thirty minutes of cardio as soon as possible and extend that time as your fitness improves. You can do the entire routine at one time or spread your exercise throughout the day. Just be sure to log at least thirty minutes daily. Once you reach that goal, work in at least another fifteen to twenty minutes of resistance exercise.

We recommend a maximum of one hour of strenuous cardiovascular exercise per day, six days a week. The Ten Commandments direct us to take a day of rest each week, and your body needs that rest. When you exercise, your body consumes glycogen, which is the sugar stored in the muscles. Observing an "exercise Sabbath" helps the muscles replenish glycogen stores.

You may see some people in the gym who are quite advanced, working out longer than an hour between their cardio exercises and weight training. This routine is okay under these conditions: you are combining aerobic and resistance training; you have worked up to this level over time; and it meets your specific fitness goals. However, most people do not require that much exercise; an hour a day should be more than enough to get great results.

Here's a sample exercise program based on thirty minutes of cardiovascular exercise each day. On days of longer exercise, it's all right to break your regimen into two sections, such as thirty minutes in the morning and thirty minutes later in the day. Always bookend each session with a few minutes of warmup and cool-down:

Monday	30 minutes of walking followed by stretching
Tuesday	30 minutes on an elliptical trainer (step machine)
	30 minutes of resistance exercise
Wednesday	30 minutes of walking followed by stretching
Thursday	30 minutes on a stationary bike
	30 minutes of resistance exercise
Friday	30 minutes on an elliptical trainer
Saturday	30 minutes on a stationary bike
	20 minutes of circuit training (alternating resistance exercises with two to four minutes of cardio movement, such as stepping, walking, cycling, or jumping rope)

If you do not have access to a gym, fitness center, or in-home machines such as a treadmill or elliptical trainer, don't worry. You can still follow the program. Most people who don't work out at a gym use walking as their primary form of cardiovascular exercise. You can map out a challenging course or two in your neighborhood, perhaps including some hills. Or you may want to walk laps on the local high-school track.

There are cardio alternatives to walking, however. If you have access to a bicycle, use it. Just make sure you're pedaling consistently for the entire ride, because a simple cruise through the park doesn't count for much cardio. If you are blessed to live in an area where hiking trails, canoeing or kayaking, or cross-country skiing is readily available, these are great alternatives to walking. Enjoy them! Exercise videos are another great source for at-home workouts. There are hundreds of them on the market featuring every type of workout imaginable—from step aerobics to kickboxing to Pilates.

You don't need a gym for resistance exercise either. There are many low-cost exercise tools you can use right in your own home, such as dumbbells and exercise tubing. Here's a sample workout week using home-based devices for cardio and strength training.

Monday	30 minutes of walking, core training, and stretching
Tuesday	30 minutes of walking or biking
	30 minutes of resistance training using dumbbells or exercise tubing for squats, lunges, bicep curls, and crunches, as well as push-ups, pull-ups, etc.
Wednesday	30 minutes of interval walking (meaning to alternate your pace between one minute of fast walking or jogging and two minutes at a more moderate pace), followed by core training and stretching
Thursday	30 minutes of walking or cardio workout video
	30 minutes of resistance training using dumbbells or exercise tubing

Friday	30 minutes of walking, core training, and stretching
Saturday	20 minutes of walking or biking
	30 minutes of circuit training

When you're ready for a more advanced workout, it might look like this:

Monday	45 minutes of an aerobic class, followed by stretching
Tuesday	30 minutes of fast walking plus 30 minutes of lifting weights, targeting the upper body
Wednesday	45 minutes on an elliptical trainer, followed by stretching
Thursday	30 minutes on a stationary bike plus 30 minutes lifting weights and circuit training, targeting the lower body
Friday	45 minutes of kickboxing class, followed by stretching
Saturday	30 minutes of fast walking

Find the program that works best for you, but don't be afraid to experiment. Exercise doesn't have to be difficult. Hold yourself accountable to others, such as those you run with in the neighborhood or meet at the gym, to keep you on track. Try to think of your exercise time as an adventure and challenge instead of drudgery or duty. You can serve as your own personal trainer, but if you need more specific pointers for your regimen, consult a qualified fitness expert at a local gym.

As you embark on a new or accelerated personal exercise program, take heart. God designed your body to move, so regard exercise as a form of worship to Him. It is a specific way you can honor the temple of the Holy Spirit, your body. Paul urged, "Whether, then, you eat or drink or whatever you do, do all to the glory of God" (1 Corinthians 10:31). So exercise to the glory of God and present your body to Him as a "living and holy sacrifice" (Romans 12:1).

Keys to Total Heart Health

Chapter 15: Exercising Your Way to a Healthy Heart

- The health of your heart depends on consistent physical exercise.
- Anything we do that endangers the body is disrespectful of God's temple, and should be avoided.
- A complete exercise program consists of three categories of activity: cardiovascular, resistance, and flexibility.
- Cardio exercise happens when you move your large muscle groups rhythmically and repetitively, such as in walking, running, biking, swimming laps, dancing, or stairstepping.
- Cardio exercise is always about progression. Use the FITT scale. **F** is for frequency, **I** for intensity, **T** refers to the type of exercise you do, and **T** is for the time you exercise each day. To progress, increase your exercise by one FITT component at a time.
- Resistance exercises use force on the muscles to strengthen them. Work each muscle group one to three sets of eight to twelve repetitions each. The difficulty level can range from challenge to fatigue to failure.
- Flexibility, achieved primarily through stretching, is the most neglected. All major muscle groups should be stretched one to three times a workout session, one to three sessions a week. Extend the muscle, and hold it there ten to thirty seconds.
- Minimum cardio exercise for general health is twenty minutes per day. To build more muscle, exercise a little more than thirty minutes a day, maintaining the cardio and flexibility program while adding ten to fifteen minutes of resistance exercise before or after your cardio.

16
Power with a Purpose

God pumps His energy into you for a reason,
so start using it.

Dr. Ed Young

Jim DeLoach, my associate, underwent a baptism of fire early in life. As a seventeen-year-old, he entered the United States Navy at the height of World War II. Jim was assigned to a ship in the raging Pacific war theater.

Jim recalls his first Christmas away from Alabama, where he had been raised. He was in a strange environment, on his way to battle. Excitement mingled with fear as he wondered what he would face. Jim's loved ones were far away. On that Christmas, he says now, "I cried and cried."

Jim's ship was in the thick of the battle. This young man witnessed carnage and death firsthand. One of the experiences branded on Jim's memory was that of his best friend dying in his arms. The young sailor had been burned severely, and Jim could smell the flesh burning and hear the heat crackling on the skin.

In God's providence, Jim survived the war. He had heard about the Lord as a child, but watching his buddy burn to death focused Jim's thoughts on God and the Bible's words about hell. As a young man fresh from the war, Jim opened his life to Jesus Christ and committed to serving Him full-time. I met Jim when I entered seminary. He was several years ahead of me; as a teaching assistant, Jim graded my papers and taught some classes I attended.

When I was invited to become pastor of Houston's Second Baptist Church in 1978, Jim joined the staff with me. This "Alabama country boy" proved himself as a scholar, administrator, and gifted teacher. He rose to every challenge set before him, including many critical start-up tasks ranging from managing church finances and business to establishing an effective program for visiting people in need. At one point, a young woman missionary who was a member of our church was captured by communist rebels in a dangerous African country. We sent Jim to handle the difficult chore of finalizing her release and getting her safely back to the United States.

Jim is a wonderful example of spiritual energy balance. Having opened himself to God's grace and blessing in Christ, he generously poured himself out to others. He reminds us of Christ's words in Matthew 10:8: "Freely you received, freely give." Receiving from God, or taking in spiritual fuel from Him, is vital to spiritual heart health, just as eating healthy food is vital to physical heart health. But diet—energy in—must be balanced by exercise— energy out, as Kristy Brown emphasized in the previous chapter. Similarly, having freely received from God, we must freely give of ourselves to achieve healthy spiritual energy balance.

This doesn't mean your life will necessarily look like Jim's. His loving ministry to others was the product of what God did in him and through him in light of his talents, abilities, gifts, personality, and passions. Your challenge is to funnel the energy you take in from God into service to Him and others that reflects how God made you.

Work Out What God Works In

Do you realize that God has written a spiritual workout regimen right into His Word? Here it is: "Work out your salvation with fear and trembling; for it is God who is at work in you, both to will and to work for His good pleasure" (Philippians 2:12–13). The essence of our spiritual energy is the salvation God works in us. As we feed on Him, our hearts grow strong. Why do we need a strong heart? Because God's plan is for us to direct that energy into serving others. We work out in service what God works into us through salvation. That's energy balance for the spiritual heart.

The Bible teaches us that salvation has three tenses: past, present, and future. Salvation past is called *justification*. Romans 5:1 says, "Therefore, having been justified by faith, we have peace with God through our Lord Jesus Christ." We believe that Jesus Christ is the Son of God and our only Savior and that we are sinners in need of salvation. Confessing and turning from our sin and receiving Christ, we are justified. It's a done deal, and from that moment our salvation is secured. Your justification means that as far as God the Judge is concerned, the words "Not Guilty" have been indelibly etched beside your name.

Salvation present is called *sanctification*. Paul wrote to the Thessalonian Christians, "Now may the God of peace Himself sanctify you entirely" (1 Thessalonians 5:23). These people were already justified based on their past repentance and commitment to Christ. Paul now prays for their ongoing sanctification. To be sanctified means to be set apart for God's exclusive use. It's the process of being yielded to Him increasingly. We are being sanctified as we grow and mature in the Lord.

Salvation future is called *glorification*. At the end of time, when we see Christ face-to-face, even our bodies will be transformed into "conformity with the body of His glory" (see Philippians 3:20–21). This will be the capstone to our salvation.

Salvation not only has three tenses, but it also impacts all three dimensions of our being. Justification happens in the spirit, where God "rescued us from the domain of darkness, and transferred us to the kingdom of His beloved Son" (Colossians 1:13). Sanctification occurs in the soul, as the salvation that awakened the spirit to God begins to transform our minds, wills, and emotions. And glorification impacts the body, eventuating in our ultimate transformation into Christ's likeness.

But why did God justify us? And why does God continue to "work in" His salvation through sanctification? Is it only so that we can go to heaven when we die? That is certainly a wonderful part of it. But He has worked His salvation into us so we can work out our salvation in service to Him. Jesus said, "The Son of Man did not come to be served, but to serve, and to give His life a ransom for many" (Mark 10:45). If Christ's mission was selfless service, how can ours be anything else? We are saved not just to soak up as much of God and His Word as we can on our way to heaven. We are saved to serve in the energy He continually works into us.

Not only is God responsible for the salvation He works into us, but He is also the impetus behind our "workout" for Him. Paul goes on to say in Philippians 2:13, "It is God who is at work in you, both to will and to work for His good pleasure." Willing comes before doing. Thus God is at work in you to give you the will and to empower your work.

When the Bible says God is "at work" in you, it means He's doing something that cannot be frustrated or remain half-finished. If God is involved, you know the job will get done. Paul writes, "There has never been the slightest doubt in my mind that the God who started this great work in you would keep at it and bring it to a flourishing finish on the very day Christ Jesus appears" (Philippians 1:6 MSG). Once you give Him your life by making Christ your Lord, God starts working in you and through you and won't stop until He has finished the task!

So the Holy Spirit works into us the desire, the power, and the resources to do works pleasing to God. As we say yes to what He works into us, He releases the energy, the effective working of His power within us. Spiritual heart health results as we release and channel God's energy through our ministry to others.

Your Spiritual Workout Routine

The apostle James gives us a good picture of energy balance: "If a brother or sister is without clothing and in need of daily food, and one of you says to them, 'Go in peace, be warmed and be filled,' and yet you do not give them what is necessary for their body, what use is that? Even so faith, if it has no works, is dead, being by itself" (James 2:15–17).

"Faith," in this passage, corresponds to spiritual energy in—our salvation. "Works" describes spiritual energy out—our service in Christ's name. Contrary to what much of the world assumes, good works won't save anybody. But contrary to what many Christians seem to believe, good works are a primary reason why we are saved. Paul links the two in Ephesians 2:8–10: "For by grace you have been saved through faith; and that not of yourselves, it is the gift of God; not as a result of works, so that no one may boast. For we are His workmanship, created in Christ Jesus for good works, which God prepared beforehand so that we would walk in them."

As Drs. Duncan and Leachman and Kristy Brown have reminded us, the person who eats and eats and eats but does no exercise whatsoever will get fat and flabby. In a similar way, the Christian who is always taking in—church services, Bible study meetings, sermon tapes, Christian books, and so on— and never giving out can become spiritually fat and flabby. Just as we must purposely plan plenty of physical exercise into our weekly routines to stay healthy, we must also purposely look for ways to work out our faith through selfless service to others.

Your loving service to others can be viewed as ministry in four concentric circles in your life. I want to challenge you to work out the salvation God has worked into your life, beginning at home and spreading outward to your church, your community, and the world.

Working Out at Home

No matter what your family setting—single, married, kids, no kids, close extended family—there is always plenty to be done. Whether you have a job outside the home or not, your day-to-day chores likely include fixing things at home, mowing the yard, taking out the garbage, helping with the kids, and myriad other details that keep a family functioning.

If you're single, your workout at home may be the loving service and help you offer to parents, siblings, and extended family members. If you're married, you have a wife and perhaps children who will greatly benefit from your loving care. You may not consider the mundane business of house maintenance and parenting as spiritual exercise; it's just the stuff that somebody has to do and so you get it done. But it becomes a part of your spiritual workout at home when you view it from God's perspective. The Bible says, "Let every detail in your lives—words, actions, whatever—be done in the name of the Master, Jesus, thanking God the Father every step of the way" (Colossians 3:17 MSG).

The key to spiritual exercise is in knowing for whom you are doing these tasks. For the Christian, nothing we have is really ours; it all belongs to God—including our homes and our family members. God has put these things under our care as stewards. So when you are taking your elderly parents to a doctor's appointment, you are transporting them for Jesus. The nightly ordeal of bathing the kids becomes the nightly ministry of bathing God's kids for Him. In reality, any job you do at home becomes an act of worship to God when you do it in His name.

In addition to the spiritual ministry of household tasks is the pointed spiritual ministry of sharing God and His Word with your family members. We see a beautiful template for this in the Old Testament. Moses commanded in Deuteronomy 6:6–9: "These words, which I am commanding you today, shall be on your heart. You shall teach them diligently to your sons and shall talk of them when you sit in your house and when you walk by the way and when you lie down and when you rise up. You shall bind them as a sign on your hand and they shall be as frontals on your forehead. You shall write them on the doorposts of your house and on your gates."

Christian education is the family's responsibility before it's the church's responsibility. More than anything you say, those around you are going to see God in how you live. Who God is and what God does and says also become transferable when they are part of the daily conversation in your home. Make it a point to share as a husband and a dad what God teaches you in your daily devotions, Bible studies, and sermons. Challenge your children to memorize Bible verses to recite and discuss at mealtimes—and offer prizes! When a child talks to you about a problem or a hurt, pray with him right on the spot so he learns that you include God in everything that concerns you. In short, anything you can do to keep God and His Word visible and approachable in your family is healthy spiritual exercise.

Working Out at Church

Mrs. L. G. Gates was my English teacher in junior high school in my hometown of Laurel, Mississippi. She taught me how to diagram sentences and recite poems like "The Rhyme of the Ancient Mariner." But the most important thing Mrs. Gates did for me as an eleven-year-old was to lead me to accept Jesus Christ as my Savior.

It happened at vacation Bible school one summer. I didn't really want to go, but my mother insisted. Besides, I heard about some of the activities that were planned and got excited about attending. VBS always concluded with a commencement ceremony in "big church." I was in line with the other kids when Mrs. Gates suddenly called me away from the group. She talked to me about Jesus and led me in a prayer inviting Jesus into my life.

Some years ago, Jo Beth and I were visiting in Laurel, and someone told me that Mrs. Gates, then in her nineties, had slipped into a coma. I hadn't been home in a long time, but I told my friends and relatives, "I'm going to see Mrs. Gates. She may not know me, but she will hear me."

When I got to her bedside, I drew close to her ear and spoke her name. Then I quoted a few lines of poetry I remembered from junior high. I told her who I was and thanked her for what she had done for me. Then I quoted the words so dear to her—and to me: "For God so loved the world, that he gave his only begotten Son, that whosoever believeth in him should not perish, but have everlasting life" (John 3:16 KJV).

Thank God this dear saint found a place of ministry in our church. If she hadn't, perhaps I would not be writing this book today!

The church you attend is not just a "spiritual restaurant" where you go each week to get fed. If you go to church only to take in, you are missing out on at least 50 percent of the health benefit God has for you there. You are also called to exercise your faith in your church by ministering to others with the gifts, talents, and passion God supplies to you. Whether you serve in Sunday school or vacation Bible school, in the choir or praise band, on a church board or committee, in the drama ministry, on the visitation team, or on the cleanup committee, don't miss these vital fields of ministry available at your church.

Working Out in the Community

The next circle for working out your faith is the community in which you live. A few years back, people in our church took the exercise of community ministry to a new dimension.

A tropical storm dumped torrents of rain on parts of Houston—mainly in areas where lower-income people lived. Flood damage was extreme. I visited one home where the mother was still in semishock. She walked us through the little house, showing where the water had crept up the walls. She took us into the living room and ran her hands along the mantel, demonstrating how she had clung to it to keep the waters from carrying her away.

In the aftermath, we decided to mobilize our church to aid flood victims. Many of our people gave up their evenings and weekends, and during the day numbers of people were involved. They helped with cleanup, ripped out soggy carpet, repainted walls, and took on small carpentry tasks. In keeping with

Colossians 3:17, our church's ministry to these people was performed in Christ's name.

America thrives on volunteerism. Every community has hospitals, PTAs, youth and children's organizations, homeless shelters, soup kitchens, orphanages, homes for battered women and unmarried mothers, and pregnancy centers. For the sake of the needy people in your community and for the sake of your spiritual health, find a place of service nearby and minister there with the energy God works into you! Jesus promises, "Whenever you did one of these things to someone overlooked or ignored, that was me—you did it to me" (Matthew 25:40 MSG).

Working Out in the World

The whole world is full of need, so Jesus called us to share the gospel with the whole world. Another facet of your spiritual energy out should be focused on the church's mission to the world. Not all Christians are called to be overseas missionaries, but we all are called to be missionaries where we live and to support the missionary work of others across the world. Pastor Rick Warren writes, "Telling others how they can have eternal life is the greatest thing you can do for them . . . We have the greatest news in the world, and sharing it is the greatest kindness we can show to anyone."[1]

What about your job? God has placed you there as a missionary. You are the only "pastor" some of the people you work with may even have. Be alert to their pains and crises, and be ready to minister to them. Start a prayer group or a Bible study before work or during lunch break. Make your work space a ministry center!

A friend of mind was a management consultant for the county tax collecting office. He began to build relationships with other Christians in the government agency. There was an urgent need for prayer as the tax office underwent major changes through the leadership of a new chief executive. My friend and his associates also wanted to see their colleagues receive Christ. So they started a prayer group called "The Fellowship of Levi," named after the Bible's most famous tax collector, Levi, also known as Matthew. They met every Thursday for lunch and prayer, interceding for the agency and for individual employees.

Even if you never travel outside your community to share the gospel, supporting the work of those who do is excellent spiritual exercise. Give generously to missions organizations that are taking the good news to the four corners of the world. Pray diligently for evangelists, missionaries, and their families by name. And whenever you have the opportunity, go in person, such as when signing up for a short-term missions project.

You may be saying, "I just don't have the energy for exercise, either physical or spiritual. I'm doing well just to get to church on Sunday and read my Bible occasionally." You may lack the energy you need for ministry to others because you are skimping on your spiritual diet. Italian poet Antonio Porchia observed, "A full heart has room for everything, and an empty heart has room for nothing."[2]

Make sure you are feeding regularly on God's Word. Be constant in prayer and worship. If you don't take in spiritual fuel, you'll quickly tire in your service to others. But if you are allowing God to work into your life His strength, you will have plenty of go-power for working it out in ministry.

Chapter 16: Power with a Purpose

- Having freely received from God, we must freely give of ourselves to achieve healthy spiritual balance. Funnel the energy you take in from God into service to Him and others.

- The Bible teaches that salvation has three tenses:

  1. Justification is salvation past, Christ saving you.

  2. Sanctification is salvation present, the process of being yielded to Him increasingly.

  3. Glorification is salvation future, the transformation of our bodies into a quality like Christ's at the end of time.

- Just as a person who eats and never exercises gets flabby, the Christian who always takes and never gives can become spiritually flabby.

- Your loving service to others should encompass four concentric circles:

  1. *Your Home.* More than anything you say, family members are going to see God in how you live.

  2. *Your Church.* You not only go to church to take in, but you are also called to exercise your faith in your church by ministering to others.

  3. *Your Community.* Find a place of service in your community and minister there with the energy God works into you.

  4. *The World.* We are all called to be missionaries where we live and to support the work of missionaries across the world.

17

The Buck for Your Healthy Diet Stops Here

Who should determine what you eat
and what you don't? You!

Dr. Michael Duncan and Dr. Richard Leachman

Like many men, perhaps you have received a heart health wake-up call. Perhaps a standard blood workup revealed that your cholesterol count was headed for the upper atmosphere. Suspicious chest pains may have prompted you to make that doctor's appointment you have been putting off for months—or years. Maybe for you it was the embarrassing experience of not being able to snap your favorite pair of jeans without sucking in your gut, only to have the snap come apart when you exhale. Or perhaps it was a comment from someone like, "Hey, Art, are you bulking up a little?" or "Gee, Uncle Bob, your belly is huge!"

Many people today, including heart doctors like us, have received heart health wake-up calls something like these. And the response usually includes paying closer attention to diet. Whether it's the threat of a heart attack or a wardrobe that no longer fits, people realize they aren't eating right and decide to make changes. The big decision then involves what those changes look like. How much and how often shall I eat? Which diet is right for me?

There has been an evolution in thinking about diets in the United States during the past twenty-five to thirty years. As medical science began to learn more about the link between what we eat and our overall health, new dietary guidelines were published. And with each new wrinkle in dietary health came a popular new diet—or several new diets—telling the public what to eat and

173

what to avoid. And large numbers of the population accepted these new approaches as gospel.

But as we continued to learn more about food and health, diets that were once touted as the cure-all for heart problems and unwanted pounds seemed to go out of style like clothing fashions and hairstyles. Then another diet fad would spring up, and people flocked to the bookstores for the "answer" to their health and fitness needs. During the past few decades, it has seemed as if there is a secret plot afoot in our country to devise an unending stream of new diets just to sell new books, diet foods, and exercise machines.

Marketing strategies aside, how do we know which diet is right for us? How can we sort through all the marketing hype to find an eating plan that goes beyond fashion, fad, and fiction to being both factual and fruitful in our pursuit of Total Heart Health?

In this chapter, we will answer these questions in two ways. First, we will look at a number of the kinds of diets that have evolved during the years and are still popular today in many forms. Second, we will review and crystallize the Total Heart Health approach to diet so you can evaluate and plan your personal heart health strategy.

Eat No Evil

During the 1970s, the American Heart Association and most cardiologists told people to adhere to a diet low in saturated fat and cholesterol, assuring us that such a diet would lower the risk of blocked arteries and heart attacks. While this recommendation was logical and based on scientific evidence, the food and diet industry seemed to overreact. *Fat* and *cholesterol* became four-letter words, convincing the consuming public that all fat is bad.

As a result, the market was flooded with a seemingly unending variety of low-fat foods. This gave rise to a new problem. People began eating low-fat foods in great quantities as if they had nothing more to worry about. The focus of dietary strategy became *what* we eat instead of *how much* we eat. The subliminal message was, "As long as it's low in fat, you can eat as much as you want." But this approach compromised the benefits of the low-fat diet. It doesn't take a dietician to figure out that a double scoop of "50 percent less fat" ice cream does at least as much damage as one scoop of the regular stuff.

The other problem with the focus on fat was that it overlooked other elements posing a danger to heart health, such as excessive calories and carbohydrates. This was literally a fatal error, as evidenced by the clear statistical trend toward increased obesity in our country since the 1970s.

As the pendulum of thought swung back, carbohydrates became another big target of diets. The idea of decreasing carbohydrates in the diet was a logical one, since the low-fat message resulted in people's increasing their calorie intake from carbohydrates. For example, a meat-and-potatoes eater might cut back on roast beef to avoid fat and fill the void on his plate with another serving of mashed potatoes. The low-carb message went the other way: cut back on carbs—such as potatoes, pasta, breads, and sugar—and load up on protein, which meant meat and saturated fat. Again, there was no clear message from health authorities that total calories are the major issue in the diet.

A valid criticism among medical authorities of low-carb, high-protein, high-fat diets is that they are unbalanced. By drastically reducing or eliminating carbohydrates from the diet, an important food group is being ignored. This food group, in the form of fruits, vegetables, and whole-grain foods, contains many valuable nutrients essential to a healthy diet, specifically vitamins and minerals not present in a diet of high protein and fat.

The low-carb, high-protein diet has also been criticized as unhealthy because it may result in increased cholesterol values even as participants are losing weight. Another concern is the potential negative effect of a high-protein diet on kidney function.

Finally, an unbalanced diet, such as some of the fad diets targeting or eliminating food groups, is difficult to maintain long term. Any diet, even one based on a healthy balance of food groups, is a challenge of discipline over time. Further drastic restrictions only make it more difficult to establish and sustain a strict dietary lifestyle.

These points on fad diets are underscored in a recent study reported in the *Journal of the American Medical Association*. After one year, there was no difference in weight loss among participants adhering to the low-carbohydrate diet (Atkins); the low-glycemic diet (Zone); the very low-fat diet (Ornish); and the low-calorie/small portion size diet (Weight Watchers). Almost 50 percent of the participants in each diet had dropped out of the study by twelve months, and for those who adhered to the diet, the weight loss was only ten to twelve pounds.[1]

Losing weight and maintaining weight loss are difficult for most people. The best treatment for obesity or being overweight is prevention, through modest yet persistent restriction of calorie intake in conjunction with a regular exercise program and spiritual/behavioral medication as presented by Dr. Young.

So which of the fad diets is best for you? Probably none of them. We have a better idea.

Eating with Balance

The Total Heart Health eating plan represents a balanced and reasonable approach to maintaining maximum health and a weight you can live with. The following is a focused summary of what we have been saying about diet in this book.

Calories

First and foremost, we recognize that total calorie consumption is the key to weight control. The average American consumes about 3,500 calories per day, which is twice the amount most people require to maintain normal body weight. Daily exercise is important and can help burn some of the excess calories. But even a full exercise program cannot fully compensate for a diet in which calories are out of control. We recommend a diet of 1,300 to 2,000 calories per day for most people, depending on the energy requirements of your lifestyle and activities.

Carbohydrates

We generally agree with many diets that recommend reducing or eliminating simple sugars from the diet. We're talking about cutting back or cutting out all types of sugary soft drinks, cookies, cakes, sugar, potatoes, refined breads, and other foods with a high glycemic index. However, we encourage consumption of vegetables, fruits, and whole grains, which are lower on the glycemic index and contain valuable dietary components such as fiber, vitamins, and minerals.

Protein

We recommend about one gram of protein per kilogram of ideal body weight. Your kilogram weight is your weight in pounds divided by 2.2. For example, if your ideal weight for your height is 150 pounds, you need about sixty-eight grams of protein per day. The problem is that most of us eat too much red meat for our protein needs, loading us up with high amounts of saturated fat. We recommend eating more fish and plant protein sources, which have fewer bad fats and contain other beneficial nutrients.

Fats

We recommend eating fewer foods with saturated fats (animal fats, dairy products) and trans fats and increasing consumption of polyunsaturated fats, which are present in fish and vegetable oils (except tropical oils). Trans fats are especially difficult to eliminate because they are so prevalent in many of the foods we eat, such as fried foods, packaged foods, and baked goods. You will need to employ great diligence to recognize foods with trans fats and avoid them. Remember: the terms "hydrogenated" and "partially hydrogenated," sometimes seen on nutrition labels, are synonymous with "trans fat."

Fiber

We recommend thirty-eight grams of fiber per day for adult men and twenty-five grams per day for adult women as a way to slow the digestive process and decrease the glycemic index of foods in the diet. Fiber assists in weight control by helping to curb hunger. Primary sources of fiber are whole grains and vegetables.

Sodium and Potassium

We recommend a maximum of 2,300 milligrams of sodium per day, which equates to about one teaspoon of salt. Individuals with high blood pressure, African-Americans, and older adults should try to limit sodium intake to no more than 1,500 grams per day. This group should also aim at an intake of 4,700 milligrams of potassium per day by eating potassium-rich foods such as fruits and vegetables. Like trans fats, salt can be found in many of the packaged foods we buy at the supermarket. It is wise to read the

"Nutrition Facts" panel on food boxes and wrappers to help you avoid foods with high sodium content.

What will a menu plan based on these recommendations look like? In chapter 20, we have provided a three-week menu plan based on a target of approximately 1,600 calories per day. This plan is primarily designed to help overweight and obese persons lose weight through reduced calorie intake coupled with daily exercise. However, a 1,600-calorie diet may be too drastic a step for your lifestyle and health goals. So we recommend that you use this menu plan as a guideline for the varieties of healthy foods to include in your diet while tailoring the plan to suit you by increasing portion sizes and/or adding into the plan higher-calorie foods. As always, before embarking on a new diet plan, make an appointment to talk to your doctor about it.

There are just as many plans in circulation for your spiritual heart as there are diets for your physical heart. Dr. Young will help you sort through the advice of today's pop psychologists to discover what is helpful and harmful to Total Heart Health.

Keys to Total Heart Health

Chapter 17: The Buck for Your Healthy Diet Stops Here

- The best treatment for obesity and being overweight is prevention through modest yet persistent restriction of calorie intake in conjunction with a regular exercise program and spiritual/behavioral modification.

- First and foremost, we recognize that total calorie consumption is the key to weight control. We recommend a diet of 1,300 to 2,000 calories per day for most people, depending on personal energy requirements.

- We generally agree with many diets that recommend reducing or eliminating simple sugars from the diet, those with a high glycemic index. However, we encourage consumption of vegetables, fruits, and whole grains, which have a lower glycemic index.

- We recommend about a gram of protein per kilogram of ideal body weight. Eat more fish and plant protein sources.

- We recommend eating fewer foods with saturated fats and trans fats, and increasing consumption of polyunsaturated fats.

- We recommend thirty-eight grams of fiber per day for adult men.

- We recommend a maximum of 2,300 milligrams of sodium per day, about a teaspoon of salt.

18

The Many Voices Influencing Your Masculinity

Who can show you how to be a real man better than the One who made you?

Dr. Ed Young

An English teacher was explaining to his students the concept of gender association in the English language. He noted how hurricanes at one time were only given female names, and how ships and planes were usually referred to as "she." One of the students raised her hand and asked, "What gender is a computer?"

The teacher wasn't certain. So he divided the class into two groups: males in one, females in the other, and asked them to decide if a computer should be masculine or feminine. Both groups were asked to give four reasons for their recommendations.

The group of women concluded that computers should be referred to as masculine because:

1. In order to get their attention, you have to turn them on.

2. They have a lot of data but are still clueless.

3. They are supposed to help you solve your problems, but half the time, they *are* the problem.

4. As soon as you commit to one, you realize that if you had waited a little longer, you could have had a better model.

The men, on the other hand, decided that computers should definitely be referred to as feminine because:

1. No one but their creator understands their internal logic.

2. The native language they use to communicate with other computers is incomprehensible to everyone else.

3. Even your smallest mistakes are stored in long-term memory for later retrieval.

4. As soon as you make a commitment to one, you find yourself spending half your paycheck on accessories for it.[1]

As the computer debate humorously illustrates, there are many views about what it means to be a woman and what it means to be a man in today's world. The last several decades have ushered in the revival of the feminist movement and the emergence of the men's movement. Today there are a growing number of pop divas and gurus in the media trying to shape the feminine and masculine images. Just look at the magazine section in the bookstore to see the myriad periodicals catering specifically to men and to women. Articles bombard us with gender-specific advice on how to look, how to feel, and how to perform—especially sexually.

In most cases, the world's depictions of a "real man" and a "real woman" are beyond the borders of biblical truth. One of the tragic results of separation from God is that it cuts us off from our God-given identity and a true understanding of what we were created to be as men and women. Pascal said that when people choose to turn from God and His way, they become either gods or animals, seeking to satisfy their own carnality. Sadly, this observation is reflected in today's secular view of masculinity.

A World's-Eye View of Being a Man

I believe the definitions of masculinity in circulation today can be summed up in three categories. The great twentieth-century writer and Christian Malcolm Muggeridge gave us two of them, which he termed *megalomania* and *erotomania*. I would add a third way men are portrayed and shaped today: *egomania*. Each of these categories has its own gurus and role models peddling convincing ideas about what constitutes a real man. Unfortunately, tens of thousands of men fall under the spell of these concepts and, in the process, sacrifice their families and even their health. You need to guard your spiritual heart against the allure of what the world says you should be.

Megalomania: Real Men Dominate with Power

A megalomaniac is someone who is deluded by fantasies of power, wealth, or omnipotence. We're familiar with two versions of the megalomaniac portrayed as a man's man today: muscle power and mogul power.

The movie characters often played by Arnold Schwarzenegger represent the muscle-power image men are urged to embrace and fulfill. Real men are thought to dominate with physical strength, brute force, and overpowering weaponry. Envision Conan the Barbarian, the Terminator, Kalidor (*Red Sonja*), the Eraser, and Major Dutch Schaeffer (*Predator*). Or think about the characters Sylvester Stallone made famous in films like *Rambo, Rocky, Judge Dredd,* and *Get Carter.* Or think back to the last action-adventure DVD you rented. A real man is often pictured as someone who can simply outmuscle or outgun his opponents.

Donald Trump could serve as the poster boy for the mogul-power brand of megalomania attracting men today. A mogul (derived from the sixteenth-century Muslim Moghul dynasty that conquered India) is someone who rules others with money and/or influence. Trump wouldn't last ten seconds in a fight against the likes of Conan or the Terminator. But he dominates in the world of big business and high finance. You've no doubt heard of Trump Plaza, Trump Tower, Trump Castle, Trump Mansion, Trump Taj Mahal Casino, and Trump Airlines.

In the popular reality show *The Apprentice,* Donald Trump displays his brand of power in "slash and burn" interviews aimed at discovering which aspiring young apprentice is fit for a job in the Trump empire. This mogul's in-your-face demeanor is admired by many men for its display of raw corporate power in a world where Trump is Conan. In that world, social Darwinism is the rule, and it is strictly the survival of the fittest.

Men who buy into the power identity are setting up themselves for heartache and even the loss of physical health. People in power often have to acquire increasingly greater measures of power to maintain their positions of dominance. This thirst for power can reap disastrous results. The ongoing steroid scandal among professional and Olympic athletes reveals the damaging and deadly effects of "pumping up" the body to achieve physical dominance. And we've heard the tragic stories of would-be moguls who have minimized relationships and spiritual, emotional, mental, and physical health in pursuit of their business and financial goals.

The King James Version of the Bible refers to megalomaniacs as "brutish" men. The Hebrew word appearing in the Old Testament means "stupid" and "arrogant." There's hardly anyone as scary to those around him as a man drunk with power who doesn't have the sense to use power in the right way.

I heard about a prankster who gave his friend a gigantic jigsaw puzzle. The friend didn't know it, but the prankster had removed the original pieces from the box and filled it with pieces to a different puzzle. The practical joker laughed as his frustrated friend tried to assemble the puzzle to match the picture on the box top.

That's the dilemma many of us face in the struggle to be "real men." Our culture has given us the wrong box top. The "picture" of the macho man doesn't match the pieces we have to work with. God created us to be strong in many ways, but He never intended us to ride roughshod over others physically, financially, or any other way. Pursuing the power image will hurt those around us and leave us unfulfilled as men.

Jesus gave us a healthier view of masculinity, oddly enough by talking about meekness. It's the meek, He said, who would wind up with all the marbles, not the dominating megalomaniacs (see Matthew 5:5). Many equate meekness with being a wimp. But the word *meek* in New Testament Greek pictures a wild stallion under control. The power is there, but it is restrained and channeled by the bit and bridle.

Popular ideas of manhood suggest that real men throw off the controls and throw their weight around. Jesus shows us that a real man keeps his strength within proper bounds and always under his control. Jesus Himself demonstrated this trait during His earthly ministry. He was so powerful that demons cowered in His presence and angry mobs and tough Roman soldiers were in awe. Yet He was so gentle that a little child felt comfortable in His lap. Jesus calls us to be that kind of men, leaders who demonstrate their strength by serving others instead of lording it over them.

Erotomania: Real Men Are Sex Machines

Hugh Hefner introduced the "playboy philosophy" and became the guru of those who believe that a man is best understood in terms of his sexual capabilities and conquests. If Hefner was the messiah of the sexual revolution, the voice crying in the wilderness that preceded him was Dr. Alfred Kinsey. Kinsey is the granddaddy of those who define maleness in terms of sexual behavior.

Kinsey published his book *Sexual Behavior in the Human Male* in 1948. Hefner followed with *Playboy* magazine in 1953. They came at the topic from two different perspectives: Kinsey from the platform of education and research, Hefner from the world of entertainment. But their captivating message about men was the same: real men are sex machines who should take their pleasure wherever, however, and with whomever they desire.

Kinsey, a recent film starring Liam Neeson, purportedly depicts Dr. Kinsey as a hero. We shouldn't be surprised, considering that Hollywood has been a prime vehicle for disseminating the sexual revolution. But today we know that Kinsey's "scientific research" was badly flawed. His findings of such high levels of sexual activity in men were based on "interviews with hundreds of prisoners and sexual psychopaths" as Kinsey pretended to be "surveying normal citizens."[2]

Kinsey himself "was what used to be called a 'pervert,' an omnivorous sexual obsessive whose research provided cover for indulging his proclivities."[3] My father-in-law actually took a course from the infamous Dr. Kinsey at the University of Indiana. When we would kid him about sitting under "Dr. Sex," he would simply shake his head and say that Kinsey was "off his rocker."

After more than half a century under the influence of Kinsey, Hefner, and their disciples, the sad outcomes of the sexual revolution are evident throughout our culture. We have witnessed the breakdown of the family, the wide acceptance of abortion, the exploitation of women through pornography, the exploitation of children through "kiddie porn" and pedophilia, and the explosion of sexually transmitted diseases as men, and the women who enable them, live out the sexual revolution's false premise.

Instead of reveling in the fruits of the sexual revolution, society is languishing in a sexual wilderness. Hardly anybody blinks at premarital sex and homosexuality anymore. Extramarital affairs are as common as a hello in the morning. And now the avantgarde of the left wing says, "Bisexuality—that's really where the action is." It's all excused under the postmodern claim that everyone has a right to their own lifestyle.

Just how unhealthy can this distorted view of sexuality get? There is currently a groundswell of support favoring a relaxed attitude toward sex between adults and children. One writer, Judith Levine, respected in academic circles, wrote a book dealing with "the perils of protecting children from sex." This frightening attitude further perpetuates the myth that men are sexual animals with women—and even children—as their prey.

Popular culture asks, "What's wrong with sex—any kind of sex—between consenting partners of any description?" The Bible gives us the answer. Sex is something beautiful, given by God and reserved for a man and a woman committed to each other before God in marriage. God invented sex, and He is not ashamed to give us this gift in marriage to enjoy. The Bible says that adultery and fornication are wrong because they mock what God intended sex to be: an act uniting the body, soul, mind, will, spirit, and emotions of husband and wife. Sex is designed for partners to say to each other, "I belong to you exclusively."

Don't buy into the erotomania our culture foists on men. You were not created to fulfill your sexual desires indiscriminately. If you are married, direct all your sexual energies toward the woman to whom you have committed the totality of who you are. If you are single, hold those energies in reserve as a gift for the woman you will marry someday. Stepping outside God's design for you as a man will hurt your heart in more ways than you can imagine.

Egomania: Real Men Watch Out for Number One

One psychiatrist remarked that his patients today no longer suffer merely from neuroses but from narcissism. Narcissus was a character in Greek mythology who fell in love with Echo, who then broke his heart. One day, a depressed Narcissus was walking beside a stream. He peered in and saw his reflection. Narcissus was enthralled by what he saw and fell in love with himself.

That's egomania, the obsessive preoccupation with self. Egomania is another distortion of masculinity blasted at men today. Men are encouraged: put yourself first, do it your way, get what's coming to you, step on anybody who gets in your way to the top, do what's right for you, be the captain of your ship, satisfy your own ambitions, don't back down on what you want, and make your mark. Men are coached to look out for number one and warned that it's not healthy to suppress the male ego.

Men who center their lives on themselves usually turn out to be lousy husbands, dads, and friends. Other people exist for their convenience, pleasure, and advancement. When a colleague, friend, or wife no longer measures up to the egomaniac's expectations, he or she is brushed off like lint. I heard a person actually describe himself as a "selfaholic." That's an egomaniac: addicted to himself. And like any addiction, everybody around gets hurt, including the selfaholic.

Even people who are unfamiliar with the Bible see the dangers of egomania. Yet some of their answers can be as harmful as the full-blown self-addiction many men embrace.

Obliterate the self. The answer from many religious circles is to obliterate the self in order to break the selfaholic addiction. That's the message of many of the Eastern religions. Turn off the self completely so you can be detached from the suffering and pain self experiences and causes for others. But that's a ridiculous solution. If you stub your toe, would you cut off your leg to eliminate the pain if a doctor told you to? No way. The heart of the self-centered man doesn't need to be eradicated; it needs to be transformed by the heart of the selfless Savior.

Know yourself. A philosophic solution to unbridled egomania is "Know thyself," which was first proposed by Thales of Miletus in about 585 BC. This concept is based on the notion that understanding reality is based on understanding the self. The problem with the navel-gazing self-knowledge approach is that it is limited to the worldly, temporal, material environment. God and eternity are left out of the equation, and we cannot really know ourselves apart from our eternal Creator and His designs for our lives on this planet and beyond. Recent science is discovering that humans are "hard-wired" to respond to God, and one of the measures is our capacity to "transcend" or get beyond ourselves.[4] We really cannot know the self without knowing God.

Accept yourself. For decades the gurus of psychology have been telling us to accept ourselves. That was the message of Thomas Harris's bestseller in 1967, *I'm Okay, You're Okay.* But how can a man accept a self that is unacceptable— full of conflicts and contradictions, guilt and frustration, inferiority and inhibitions? The man outside of God is not okay. He needs a transformation. Only as we are changed by God into the persons He created us to be can we accept ourselves.

Express yourself. Another answer from psychology has been "Express yourself." Gurus like Dr. Benjamin Spock taught generations of parents that the goal in childrearing is not discipline but self-expression. "Let it all hang out" was a popular mantra of this movement. Yet this approach proved to be an unhealthy and inadequate response to unbridled egomania. If you have a dozen people together in a room, all of whom have been taught to express themselves, what do you have? The stage is set for clashes, confusion, jealousy, and strife. Even Spock dissociated himself from some of his ideas after witnessing this outcome.

The answer to self-centeredness is not in self-renunciation, self-realization, self-acceptance, or self-expression. So what is the biblical answer? The New Testament says it clearly: nothing more or less than self-surrender to Jesus Christ. We are called to hand back to God the self that was handed to us by our Creator.

Jesus said that if anyone wishes to be His follower, he must leave self behind (see Luke 9:23). Paul urged that we give our very selves to God as a "living sacrifice" (Romans 12:1). God's demand is absolute and ultimate: you. He doesn't ask merely for your time, your loyalty, your trust, your service, or your money. It's a call for total surrender of self. And once we agree to His terms, we begin to experience health in every area of life.

This is a great paradox: in order to find yourself, you must give yourself away. But you are never so much your own as when you are God's. Bound to Him, you walk the earth free. Low at His feet, you stand tall before everything else. Having placed yourself in the hands of the Creator of the universe, you are free to create, to love, and to live to the maximum; you are free to be all God designed you to be.

Who Will Determine Your Identity as a Man?

We can't say it more plainly than this: the foundation for spiritual heart health is God and His Word. We're talking about the God who created your soul and spirit as well as your body. He knows all about the struggles and pain of the human heart. The personalities, celebrities, and authorities you must look to first for spiritual heart health are those who are 100 percent committed to what God has to say about the heart. The books, magazines, and tapes you should consult first are those whose content is based on the Bible.

Apart from this foundation, we are left with the best thinking and reasoning humankind can offer. By God's design, human intellect is a marvelous tool, but our knowledge and perspective are so limited compared to what God knows and sees. Ephesians 4:17–18 describes people who walk in the "futility of their mind, being darkened in their understanding." Colossians 2:8 speaks of the "philosophy and empty deception . . . the tradition of men . . . the elementary principles of the world." You don't want to base the health of your spiritual heart on counsel drawn from futile, darkened, empty minds without God. You need God's perfect Word, not humanity's best guess.

The so-called experts of the masculine identity have different ways of expressing their principles, laws, notions, concepts, and ideas, but they all have the same focus: self. This preoccupation is as old as the Garden of Eden. Adam and Eve's "guru" was the serpent. Eating the forbidden fruit, Satan promised, would make them wise. They succumbed to the temptation to displace the real God from the throne of their lives and elevate themselves to that position. And humankind has suffered from spiritual heart disease ever since.

Putting self on the throne where God belongs is not the cure to the soul's ailments; rather, it is the central cause of spiritual heart disease. G. K. Chesterton, twentieth-century Christian journalist and author, was asked in an article by an editor of the *London Times*, "What is wrong today with the world?" Chesterton is said to have written back, "Dear Sir, in response to your question, 'What is wrong with the world?' I am."[5]

Become a Man's Man in the Son of Man

Any teacher who elevates the human spirit above the Holy Spirit is detracting from, not contributing to, your spiritual heart health. You can find reliable help and advice only in those who direct you back to "the Shepherd and Guardian of your souls" (1 Peter 2:25). Why should you seek Christ's counsel and healing for your heart? I can think of several reasons.

Jesus Knows You Better Than Anyone

As much as the self-help "sages" appear to understand the inner self, none of them can claim to have created you and your heart. Nothing exists that wasn't created through Jesus, writes His disciple John (John 1:3). That means you, everything about you, inside and out, physical and spiritual. John also notes that Jesus needed no one to teach Him about human nature, because "He Himself knew what was in man" (John 2:25).

The real issue behind any world-view is its authority. When the lifestyle gurus of the world expound their theories, it is reasonable to question the authority on which their claims are based. Pop psychologists, philosophers, and prophets rest on the subjective authority of the various gurus. But the Creator of the universe and of your heart offers objective truth based on His intricate knowledge of you.

Jesus Speaks the Truth About Your Heart

Sin is at the core of all spiritual heart problems. Yet none of the pop soul doctors preach, "All have sinned and fall short of the glory of God" (Romans 3:23). Failing to deal with sin in the human heart is a hindrance, not a help, to spiritual heart health. Jesus tells you the truth about your heart's problems and then offers you His lifesaving remedy: Himself.

Many helpful resources are available that will fortify your heart and help you discern the truth about life and relationships. Fill your mind with good life-coaching material based on biblical principles. Listen to Bible teaching tapes. Invite a wise, mature, trusted Christian friend to serve as your mentor and sounding board. The Bible is the ground of truth about what your heart needs, but there are many avenues through which God's Word is taught.

Jesus Sets You Free from Self-Focus So You Can Focus on Others

Self-focus, as preached in pop psychology, is a stifling prison. Egomania is the disease that results. Developmental psychologist Erik Erikson wrote about the "stagnation" of self-absorption that afflicts some people late in life. They lose "generativity," the ability to look beyond themselves to the needs of others. The self-focus that is the core of pop psychology is not healthy.

Jesus struck the healthy balance between self-focus and others-focus. Love your neighbor as you love yourself, He said (see Luke 10:27). He called it the second greatest commandment. But to fulfill this commandment, we must also fulfill the first: love God with all your heart, soul, strength, and mind. Proper equilibrium between self-love and other-love is achieved only as we place God-love first. By loving God supremely, we are liberated from the worship of self, which is deadly idolatry. Healthy self-love results when we put God at center stage in our hearts. In so doing He gives us a right perspective of love, and we begin to love others above ourselves just as Jesus loves us.

Jesus Doesn't Deny Your Guilt; He Removes It

For many of the gurus of pop psychology, philosophy, and religion, there is no objective personal guilt, only an illusion of wrongness. Jesus lays out the real problem and the real solution. We have sinned and broken God's law, and the resulting objective guilt is eternal and absolute. Our only hope for heart healing is to face our guilt by confessing our sin and receiving His innocence. When we do, Romans 8:1–4 promises, "there is now no condemnation for those who are in Christ Jesus. For the law of the Spirit of life in Christ Jesus has set you free from the law of sin and of death. For what the Law could not do, weak as it was through the flesh, God did: sending His own Son in the likeness of sinful flesh and as an offering for sin, He condemned sin in the flesh, so that the requirement of the Law might be fulfilled in us, who do not walk according to the flesh but according to the Spirit."

The gurus don't want to talk about guilt, because they can't remove it. To raise the issue brings into focus an insurmountable problem no amount of books, chatter, tapes, or rallies can overcome. All these gurus can offer you is empty philosophy, futile thinking, and deception. Jesus Christ gives you the truth that sets your heart free!

The journey to Total Heart Health is a lifelong, disciplined pursuit. As you embark upon it, we trust that you won't journey alone. If you are single, ask a trusted friend to journey with you. Consider sharing your insights and goals with an important woman in your life: sister, mother, adult daughter, or fiancée. If you are married, we trust that your wife will be a soul mate not only for your life but also for your heart health.

Chapter 18: The Many Voices
Influencing Your Masculinity

- In most cases, the world's depictions of a "real man" and a "real woman" are beyond biblical truth.

- The world's definitions of masculinity can be summed up in three categories: megalomania, erotomania, and egomania.

- Megalomania says, "Real men dominate with power." Jesus calls us to be leaders who demonstrate their strength by serving others instead of lording over them.

- Erotomania believes, "Real men are sex machines." Sex is beautiful, given by God and reserved for a man and a woman committed to each other before God in marriage. Stepping outside God's design for you as a man will hurt your heart.

- Egomania asserts, "Real men watch out for number one." The answer to self-centeredness is not in self-renunciation, self-realization, self-acceptance, or self-expression, but rather in self-surrender.

- The foundation for spiritual heart health is God and His Word, and any guru who elevates the human spirit above the Holy Spirit is detracting from, not contributing to, your spiritual heart health.

19

Are You Ready for the 90-Day Challenge?

Is "next Monday" a good time for you
to start transforming your life?

Dr. Ed Young

Before my heart episode, Jo Beth and I had a running joke around our house. It got to the point that all we had to say to provoke a good laugh was, "I'm starting Monday." Here's how it happened.

Sometimes while watching TV or leafing through a woman's magazine, Jo Beth will discover a new plan for healthier living—a fad diet or menu plan, a miracle pill, or a new workout regimen. When she related her exciting discovery to me, I would say something like, "That's great, Jo Beth. When are we going to start?" She responded resolutely, "We're starting Monday."

Well, "Monday" rarely came. The more we looked forward to it, the more the restrictions of a new plan seemed dull and boring. So we often talked ourselves into putting off the new plan a day or two. Or, if we did make it through a Monday or several days or even a week or two, our ardor soon cooled and the new plan was shelved. So whenever one of us said to the other, "How's our new plan going?" the stock answer was, "We're starting *next* Monday." We enjoyed a lot of good laughs over that line.

But after my scary heart incident, we were both highly motivated for one more "next Monday." We didn't begin a new fad plan to lose a few pounds; we launched into a new lifestyle of Total Heart Health, a lifestyle we have maintained for more than fifteen years.

What about you? You have finished the book, having perhaps highlighted or underlined many passages you want to remember and put into practice.

When will you take the vital step from *wanting* to change and *knowing* you must change to *initiating* a life-changing transformation? The first day of the workweek really is a great time to begin a lifestyle of Total Heart Health. And the day you take up the 90-Day Challenge, you will begin a life-changing process. Does next Monday work for you?

In the introduction, I invited you to consider making a Lifestyle Transformation Commitment. If you haven't done so already, now is the time to go back to that form on page xv, and set your Total Heart Health transformation in motion. Fill in the blanks and prayerfully sign your name. Select a starting date, plan your menus, and map out your physical and spiritual fitness plan. Then go for it! I underscore what I promised at the front of this book: three months from now, if you faithfully follow the Total Heart Health plan, you will look into the mirror and see a new man, healthier in spirit and body!

Change Is a Process

Whenever I make a decision to change my spiritual, dietary, or fitness habits, I often wish I could wake up the next morning and be completely transformed. But any kind of significant change in our lives is a process of five stages: pre-contemplation, contemplation, preparation, action, and maintenance.[1] In other words, before we can think about a change, we have to *think about thinking about it*. Before we take some steps, we have to make our plans. And once we make some changes, we have to maintain the new lifestyle.

The fact that you have taken time to read this book indicates that you've passed the first two stages. You're ready to make some plans and start moving forward on your 90-day track to a Total Heart Health lifestyle.

Most models of behavioral change focus on feelings, thoughts, and behavior. They often don't succeed because they ignore the fundamental power of change, which is spiritual. In this book, we have detailed a simple program for enriching your relationship with God, which is where all good health begins. However, you can have the loftiest goals for change and the best plans to get you there, but if you don't make the decision to change and follow through, transformation won't occur.

Journaling Your 90-Day Challenge

In this chapter we want to give you another tool to help you start and maintain the 90-Day Challenge. We call it the Total Heart Health Journal. You'll find sample sheets on pages 202–4.[2] Feel free to photocopy these pages or simply hand-copy the headings into the journal you already use. At the conclusion of the 90-Day Challenge, you may continue to use these pages to maintain the lifestyle you have adopted.

For each day, begin by writing in the day of the challenge (such as Day 1, Day 2, and so on), the date, or both. The headings on each journal page will help you keep track of the four key elements for the Total Heart Health lifestyle we have discussed in this book: spiritual energy in, physical energy in, spiritual energy out, and physical energy out. You may want to keep your journal with you and make entries throughout the day. Or it may work better for you to sit down with your journal at the end of the day and make the appropriate entries. Whatever method you choose, using this journal template will help you stay on track day by day.

Look at this template as a guide offering direction and encouragement instead of a law requiring obedience. Few things are less inspiring than a hard, cold directive that demands, "Do this or else!" Rather, make the Total Heart Health Journal work for you. Use only the sections that encourage you in the right direction. Allow this experience to assist you in the direction you want to go.

Spiritual Energy In

The first section will encourage you toward a strong spiritual heart. We recommend that you spend about thirty minutes a day reading from the Bible and connecting with God in prayer. Enter the reference to the Bible passage you read in the space provided. You may want to choose a book of the Bible—such as Genesis, John, Romans, or Proverbs—and read a chapter each day. You may want to skip around in the Bible, reading from a different section each day— Old Testament, New Testament, Gospels, epistles, poetry, history. If you don't know where to start reading in the Bible, consider using the ninety passages provided in chapter 21, which will take you through your 90-Day Challenge.[3]

As you read, ponder the two questions on the blank journal sheet to help you summarize what you get out of your daily reading. This is your chance to respond to what God says to you in the Bible each day. Jot down what you sense He is telling you and how you want to respond. There are no right or wrong answers here. God speaks to our hearts through His Word, so you will tap into His heart as you read. Simply summarize what you find and identify what you sense He is asking you to do.

The next section is prayer. We suggest that you use your thumb and four fingers to help you remember specific things you want to pray about. Jot down in the space provided what you pray for. When God answers that prayer in some way, write down the answer and the date. Keeping a record of answered prayer will encourage your faith and strengthen your prayer resolve.

Thumb. The thumb stands for thankfulness, just like a thumbs-up stands for "Everything's great." A grateful heart is a healthy heart emotionally and mentally. Gratitude keeps moving us forward because it reminds us of the blessings of the past. It's good to start your personal prayer time with thanks and praise.

Index finger. Your index finger is your "pointer," which we commonly use to give or confirm directions. So your pointer finger prompts you to seek God for His direction, guidance, and right decisions. Ask God each day for His direction for your life in general and specifically in the tasks and experiences you will face.

Middle finger. The middle finger is usually the tallest, reminding us to pray for those who "stand tall" in authority over us. Pray for God's provision and blessing on city, county, state, and national leaders. Pray for your pastor and other church leaders. If you work, pray for the managers in your workplace. Pray for these people by name whenever possible.

Ring finger. The ring finger represents those within your closest circle of love: your wife, children, parents, grandchildren, extended family members, and closest friends. The ring finger also reminds us of commitment. Whenever you say to someone, "I'll pray for you," you're making a commitment. Write the names of these people under this heading and fulfill your commitment to pray for them.

Pinky. Finally, your little finger symbolizes people in society who are downtrodden, neglected, defenseless, and poor. There is a special place in God's heart for the impoverished—widows, orphans, single moms, the homeless—those unable to hold productive jobs because of health issues. Pray for organizations and ministries that work to alleviate human suffering in some way.

Praying for people is a motivator to actively express love for others, especially those in need around you. James says it is not enough simply to say to a hungry person, "Be full!" (see James 2:14–17). Praying for the down and out should prompt loving, sacrificial action to lift them up and pull them in.

Physical Energy In

Dr. Mike Duncan and Dr. Rick Leachman have provided a treasure of information in this book, equipping you to implement a daily menu that is nutritious and delicious. You may choose to track your daily calorie intake in this section based on your individual calorie-need profile. You may also find it helpful to jot down what you eat each day: foods, portions, water intake, vitamins, and so on. If you decide to follow the weight-loss menu plan in chapter 20, you can summarize how you're doing here.

Spiritual Energy Out

This could be the most exciting section in your daily journal. How is God using you each day to serve the needs of others—at home, at church, in your community, in the world at large? In what ways are you working out what God has worked in your life? Were you able to help someone in distress today? Were you able to share your faith in Christ with someone who is not a Christian? Did God prompt you to stop and pray with or encourage someone today—a coworker, a family member, even a total stranger? Did God use you to brighten someone's day, lighten their load, or point them to Jesus? As you keep track of these "divine encounters" in your journal, they will keep you alert to the needs of others throughout your daily activities, allowing you to grow stronger "muscles" of faith and service.

Physical Energy Out

In chapter 15, Kristy Brown gave you valuable information to help you put together a daily exercise plan that's just right for you. She recommends a minimum of thirty minutes a day of moderate exercise six days a week. This section of your journal will guide you in recording how well you do each day at staying with the regimen you have decided to follow.

A Total Heart Health Lifestyle

What happens at the end of your 90-Day Challenge? Commencement. When we were in school, we thought *commencement* meant "the end," didn't we? No more classes, textbooks, or homework. But we now know that the word *commencement* means the beginning, not the end. When you graduated from high school or college, you *commenced* a productive life in your chosen field. In the same way, the last day of your 90-Day Challenge is your commencement of a fulfilling, rewarding, and satisfying lifestyle of Total Heart Health. Jo Beth and I have stayed with the program for more than fifteen years, so we know you can do it!

We could leave you with any number of worn-out motivational clichés: "The journey of a thousand miles begins with a single step"; "If it is to be, it is up to me"; "Today is the first day of the rest of your life." But we believe that the promise and potential of a Total Heart Health lifestyle are no better summarized than in these words from the apostle Paul. This is our heartfelt prayer and hope for you:

> May God himself,
> the God who makes everything holy and whole,
> make you holy and whole,
> put you together—spirit, soul, and body—
> and keep you fit for the coming of our Master, Jesus Christ.
> (1 Thessalonians 5:23 MSG)

Keys to Total Heart Health

Chapter 19: Are You Ready
for the 90-Day Challenge?

- When will you take the vital step from *wanting* to change and *knowing* you must change to *initiating* life-changing transformation? The day you take up the 90-Day Challenge, you will begin a life-changing process!

- Most models of behavioral change focus on feelings, thoughts, and behavior. They don't often succeed because they ignore the fundamental power of change, which is spiritual.

- You can have the loftiest goals for change and the best plans to get you there, but if you don't make the decision to change and follow through, transformation won't occur.

- The Total Heart Health Journal, included here, will help you get started on the 90-Day Challenge. For a more detailed plan of action, get *The Total Heart Health for Men Workbook* (Thomas Nelson, 2005).

- We recommend you spend about thirty minutes a day reading from the Bible and connecting with God in prayer. A helpful tool is *Daily Strength for Total Heart Health* (Thomas Nelson, 2005).

- Use the information in this book to implement a daily menu that is nutritional and delicious.

- Track your involvement in ministering to and serving others.

- Give thirty minutes a day to physical exercise, following the valuable information provided in chapter 15.

Total Heart Health Journal

Day _____

SPIRITUAL ENERGY IN

Today's Bible Passage _____

What do you sense God is saying to you in the passage you read?

How will you respond to God's message to you today?

Today's "Hand" Prayer

Thumb: Tell God what you are thankful for.

Index Finger: Pray for God's direction in your life and in the lives of others.

Middle Finger: Pray for those in authority in your church, country, workplace, and so on.

Ring Finger: Pray for your spouse, children, family members, close friends, and so on.

Pinky: Pray for the poor, neglected, oppressed, and abused.

PHYSICAL ENERGY IN

Note your food intake today under the headings you want to track:

Approximately how many calories did you take in today?

What did you eat today?

    Breakfast

    Lunch

    Dinner

    Snacks

What was your water intake today (six twelve-ounce glasses recommended)?

Did you take your vitamins/supplements/medications today?

SPIRITUAL ENERGY OUT

In what ways did you exercise your faith today in loving service to others?

    In your home:

    In your church:

    In your community:

    In the world:

PHYSICAL ENERGY OUT

Note the exercise you accomplished today under the headings you want to track.

Total time spent exercising (minimum of thirty minutes recommended):

Type and time of cardiovascular exercise:

Type and time of resistance (strength) exercise:

Type and time of flexibility (stretching) exercise:

Did you allow time for warmup and cool-down?

What is your weight today?

Photocopy these sample pages for your own Total Heart Health journal.

Physical Energy In: Menus and Recipes

Twenty-one days of easy, healthy weight-loss menus
for you and your family.

The menus we share with you capture the wholesome goodness of common
foods in delicious, easy-to-prepare meals in portions that will help you lose
weight. These meals are rich in fruits, vegetables, and whole grains, making
them high in fiber and low in saturated fats and trans fats. Each daily menu
averages approximately 1,600 calories. If your dietary plan requires more
calories, you may increase the serving sizes or include foods that up the
calorie count. Be sure to talk to your doctor before starting this or any other
diet plan.

The following table breaks down the daily average distribution of metabolic fuels and other important nutrients.

Total Heart Health Menus
Nutrition Summary
Daily Average 1,587 Calories

Protein	97 grams	22 percent of calories
Carbohydrates	197 grams	48 percent of calories
Fats	54 grams	30 percent of calories
Fiber	30 grams	
Sodium	2,234 mg	
Potassium	2,855 mg	

As with all low-calorie diets, however, these menus may not fulfill all the recommended intakes for certain nutrients according to the National Academies of Sciences. So we recommend that those who embark on this eating plan supplement their diet with one multivitamin and 600 mg of calcium daily.

These menus provide the weekly amount of omega-3 fatty acids recommended by the American Heart Association by including seafood at least twice a week.[1] However, persons with chronic illnesses such as heart disease and autoimmune disorders should receive 1,000 mg of omega-3 fatty acids per day, which usually requires three to five capsules of fish oil supplement daily.

It should be noted that not all condiments used in these menus are fat-free, notably the salad dressings. We caution you not to use all fat-free condiments when the meal itself is generally low in fat, because nutrient absorption will be negatively affected. A recent study in the *American Journal of Clinical Nutrition* revealed that substantially greater absorption of carotenoids (lycopene, alpha and beta carotene) was observed when salads were consumed with full-fat rather than reduced-fat salad dressing.

These menus and recipes are relatively low in sodium. If salt or salty foods, such as bouillon, are added in the food preparation, daily sodium intake will be higher.

General Menu Guidelines

As you use the weight-loss menus we provide, here are some important guidelines to keep in mind.

Servings. Unless otherwise noted, these menus are presented in servings for one person. If others in your household are following this plan, simply add servings for them.

Eggs. Eggs are a good source of protein and are included in several breakfast menus. But eggs should be prepared without fat, such as boiled, poached, or fried in fat-free cooking spray. We recommend that you use omega-3 enriched eggs whenever possible, such as Eggland's Best, EggsPlus, or Christopher Eggs.

Bread and cereal products. Whenever this menu calls for bread, toast, crackers, dinner rolls, and the like, we recommend 100 percent whole-grain products that provide at least three grams of fiber per serving. As for breakfast cereals, buy low-fat, whole-grain hot and cold cereals that contain at least four grams of fiber per serving.

Sweeteners. If you wish to sweeten menu items such as dry or cooked cereal, we recommend a calorie-free sugar substitute. But stay informed about possible side effects from non-nutritive sweeteners.

Spreads. If you wish to add a buttery spread to bread or cooked vegetables, we recommend a butter substitute, such as imitation butter flakes. Butter sprays should be limited to five doses per serving to limit calories.

Fresh fruit. Whenever a menu calls for "1 fresh fruit," you may use one of the following: one medium orange, apple, peach, nectarine, or pear; one-half grapefruit; one-half cantaloupe; one cup melon chunks; two small plums or kiwis; one cup strawberries; one-half cup other berries (blueberries, raspberries, blackberries); one small banana; one cup grapes (freeze them for fun!); or one-half cup fresh pineapple or canned pineapple in its own juice.

Raw vegetables. Whenever a menu suggests a snack of raw veggies, one serving is filled with either two stalks of celery, six baby carrots, one medium green pepper, one medium tomato, or other vegetables in equivalent amounts.

Fish. Whenever a menu entrée features fish, we recommend red snapper, sole, tilapia, flounder, albacore, or salmon. Whenever possible, use cold-water fish instead of farm raised.

Beverages. No beverages are included in these menus, nor are they included in the daily averages for calorie intake. An important part of a healthy daily diet is water intake—approximately six twelve-ounce glasses per day. Drinking a glass of water with each meal is one way to help you fulfill that need. If you prefer other beverages with meals and snacks, such as coffee, tea, and soda, we recommend sugar-free varieties.

Day 1

Breakfast   1 cup cooked oatmeal with skim milk and 2 tsp honey

Add 2 tbsp chopped walnuts, 2 tbsp ground flaxseed

1 fresh fruit

Lunch   Chicken Caesar salad

3 oz grilled chicken strips, 3 cups romaine lettuce, 1 tbsp Parmesan cheese, 2 tbsp Caesar salad dressing, 1 tbsp plain croutons

2 large high-fiber crackers (e.g., Ry Krisp)

Snack   1 fresh fruit

Dinner   4 oz seared or grilled salmon with 2 tbsp barbecue sauce

¼ cup brown rice cooked with 1 tbsp olive oil

1 cup cooked broccoli, cauliflower, and carrots sprinkled with lemon juice

1 tomato broiled with 1 tbsp Parmesan cheese on top

Snack   ½ cup instant pudding made with skim or low-fat milk

1 fresh fruit

Day 2

Breakfast	2 eggs
	2 slices toast
	1 fresh fruit
Lunch	Turkey and spinach wrap
	1 whole-wheat low-carb tortilla, 3 oz turkey breast meat, ½ cup baby spinach leaves, 1 tbsp light dressing
	Raw veggies
	1 fresh fruit
Snack	1 oz low-fat cheese
	2 large high-fiber crackers
Dinner	1 serving Beef and Broccoli Sauté*
	½ cup brown rice, steamed or cooked in water or broth
	Salad with mixed greens and assorted raw vegetables
	2 tbsp oil and vinegar dressing
Snack	½ cup sherbet

---

*Beef and Broccoli Sauté (serves 4)

¾ lb lean beef strips	4–5 cups broccoli pieces
1 tbsp olive oil	6 cloves minced garlic
1 tsp sesame oil	2 tbsp cooking sherry
1 tbsp soy sauce	1½ tbsp ginger root
½ tsp red pepper flakes	

Sauté garlic in olive oil, add other ingredients, and cook until meat is done and broccoli is al dente.

Day 3

Breakfast   1 cup cereal with skim milk and 2 tbsp ground flaxseed

1 slice toast

1 fresh fruit

Lunch   Fish salad

3 oz water-packed tuna or sardines, 1 tsp lemon juice, 1 tbsp pickle relish, 1 tbsp creamy mustard

4 large or 12 small crackers

Raw veggies

1 fresh fruit

Snack   ¼ cup unsalted roasted almonds

2 tbsp raisins or chopped dates

Dinner   1 grilled chicken breast marinated in teriyaki sauce

1 small baked potato plain or with butter substitute and 1 tbsp brown sugar

½ cup spinach sautéed in olive oil and chopped garlic

1 whole-wheat roll

1 fresh fruit

Snack   1 fudge Popsicle

Day 4

Breakfast	Fruit smoothie
	Blend 6 oz silken tofu, ⅔ cup berries, 1 cup apple juice, 1 tsp vanilla, 1 small banana.
	2 slices toast
Lunch	Chinese takeout
	1½ cup moo goo gai pan (chicken and vegetables in white sauce), ½ cup white steamed rice, 1 cup soup
Snack	1 fresh fruit
Dinner	5 oz grilled beef tenderloin fillet
	½ cup French-style green beans with slivered almonds browned in butter
	1 serving Fake-Out Mashed Potatoes*
Snack	1 frozen fruit juice bar

---

*Fake-Out Mashed Potatoes (serves 4)

1 head cauliflower broken into florets   ¼–½ cup skim milk

Butter substitute   Low fat sour cream (optional)

Steam cauliflower until soft. Blend in food processor, adding milk until cauliflower reaches the consistency of mashed potatoes. Add butter substitute, salt, and pepper to taste. Serve with a dollop of low-fat sour cream if desired.

Day 5

Breakfast	1 egg
	4 4-inch whole-wheat pancakes with 3 tbsp syrup
	1 fresh fruit
Lunch	1 cup low-fat, low-sodium soup
	Turkey sandwich
	2 slices bread, 4 oz turkey, 1 slice nonfat cheese, lettuce, 1–2 tomato slices, 1 tsp mustard
Snack	Raw veggies
Dinner	4 oz grilled or baked fish fillet, seasoned to taste
	½ cup brown rice
	5 asparagus spears steamed and sprinkled with lemon juice
	1 broiled tomato with low-fat feta cheese on top
	1 dinner roll
Snack	6 oz low-fat vanilla yogurt
	1 fresh fruit

Day 6

Breakfast	1 breakfast wrap
	2 scrambled eggs, 1 oz shredded low-fat cheese, ⅓ cup hash-browned potatoes rolled in a whole-wheat tortilla
Lunch	1 cup low-fat cottage cheese
	1 tomato
	2 green onions
	7 crackers
Snack	1 fresh fruit
Dinner	1 serving Chicken Fajita Salad and Rice*
	1 oz baked corn tortilla chips
Snack	¼ cup unsalted dry-roasted peanuts

---

*Chicken Fajita Salad and Rice (serves 4)

1 lb chicken breast strips	Fajita (or taco) seasoning
1 sliced onion	1 sliced green pepper
1 cup brown rice	1 cup pico de gallo

Marinate chicken strips 4–6 hours in seasoning. Make pico de gallo by mixing chopped onions, tomatoes, and cilantro with lemon juice and salt to taste.

Sauté marinated chicken strips with sliced onion and pepper. Cook brown rice, adding a small amount of the seasoning to the water. Serve chicken mixture over rice, topped with pico de gallo.

Day 7

Breakfast	Open-faced turkey and cheese melt
	On each slice of bread: 1-oz slice turkey and 1 slice fat-free cheese. Broil until cheese is melted.
	1 fresh fruit
Lunch	Shrimp salad
	4 oz cooked shrimp served with cocktail sauce and lemon juice on a bed of greens
	2 large or 6 regular crackers
Snack	6 oz low-fat fruity yogurt with ¼ cup low-fat granola cereal
Dinner	1 roasted Cornish game hen
	1 cup steamed broccoli sprinkled with lemon juice
	1 serving Baked Sweet Potato Wedges*
Snack	½ cup low-fat ice cream

---

*Baked Sweet Potato Wedges (serves 4)

Cut two large sweet potatoes lengthwise into wedges, skin on. Sprinkle with substitute butter, salt, and other spices to taste (curry, tarragon, thyme). Bake 30 minutes at 375 degrees or until brown and cooked through.

Day 8

Breakfast	6 oz low-fat yogurt mixed with 2 tbsp chopped walnuts and 2 tbsp ground flaxseed
Lunch	Salmon salad in whole-wheat pita bread
	Mix and stuff into pita 3 oz canned salmon, 1 chopped hard-boiled egg, 1 tbsp creamy mustard, 1 tbsp low-fat mayonnaise or salad dressing, 1 tbsp sweet pickle relish, ½ chopped apple.
Snack	Raw veggies
Dinner	1 serving Quick and Easy Black Bean Soup*
	1¼ cup green salad, sliced tomatoes, or other raw veggies with 2 tbsp olive oil and vinegar dressing
	5 unsalted saltine crackers
	1 fresh fruit
Snack	¼ cup unsalted dry roasted peanuts

---

*Quick and Easy Black Bean Soup (serves 6)

2 tbsp canola oil	½ cup chopped carrots
½ cup chopped celery	1 chopped onion
2 tbsp chopped green chilies	1 tsp ground cumin
2 14.5-oz cans diced tomatoes, no salt	½ cup chopped cilantro
3 15-oz cans black beans with juice	1 11-oz can whole-kernel corn, no salt

Heal oil in a large pot over medium heat. Add carrots, celery, and ½ cup onion; cook until tender. Add remaining ingredients except cilantro and remaining onion. Bring to a boil. Reduce heat and simmer 20 minutes. Top each serving with cilantro and chopped onion. Freeze leftovers in one-serving sizes for later meals.

Day 9

Breakfast	1 cup cereal with skim milk and 2 tbsp ground flaxseed
	½ cup berries
	1 slice toast
Lunch	Sub sandwich
	6" whole-grain roll, 3 oz turkey, fresh veggie toppings, oil and vinegar dressing, pepper
	1½ oz baked wheat chips
Snack	1 fresh fruit
	1 oz mozzarella cheese stick
Dinner	4 oz roasted pork tenderloin brushed with olive oil, chopped garlic, thyme, and pepper
	3 small new potatoes halved and roasted with meat
	1 cup steamed broccoli sprinkled with lemon juice
	½ cup cooked carrots seasoned with basil and olive oil
Snack	1 fresh fruit

Day 10

Breakfast	2 slices toast with 2 tbsp peanut butter and 2 tsp honey or jelly
	1 fresh fruit
Lunch	1½ cups leftover Quick and Easy Black Bean Soup
	10 unsalted saltine crackers
Snack	1 fresh fruit
Dinner	1 Taco Salad in Baked Tortilla Bowl*
Snack	1 fresh fruit

---

*Taco Salad in Baked Tortilla Bowl

4 oz lean ground turkey	1 tbsp taco spices
½ chopped avocado	½ chopped tomato
2 tbsp sour cream	1 oz shredded nonfat cheese
1 whole-wheat tortilla	Mixed greens

Line bottom and sides of ovenproof bowl with tortilla, bake at 350 degrees for 10–12 minutes. Cook turkey with taco spices. Fill tortilla bowl with greens, top with meat, avocado, tomato, sour cream, and cheese. And you can eat the bowl!

Day 11

Breakfast   Omelet with 2 eggs, mushrooms, onions, tomatoes, 1 oz shredded low-fat cheese

4 oz fruit juice

Lunch   Toasted chicken salad sandwich

Mix and spread between two slices of toast 3 oz canned chicken, 2 tbsp chopped celery, 1 tbsp chopped onion, 2 tbsp low-fat mayonnaise or salad dressing. Add two tomato slices and lettuce.

Snack   2 tbsp raisins

Dinner   Marinated and Grilled Flank Steak*

1 corn on the cob, boiled and unsalted

Mixed green salad with assorted raw veggies with oil and vinegar dressing

1 fresh fruit

Snack   ½ cup fat-free pudding

---

*Marinated and Grilled Flank Steak (serves 4)
Marinade:

⅓ cup dry red cooking wine   ½ cup chopped sweet onion

1 tbsp lite soy sauce   3 cloves minced garlic

Marinate 1-pound flank steak up to 24 hours and grill to desired tenderness.

Day 12

Breakfast 1 cup cooked oatmeal with skim milk and 2 tsp honey

Add 2 tbsp chopped walnuts, 2 tbsp ground flaxseed

1 fresh fruit

Lunch Grilled chicken salad

4 oz grilled chicken breast strips, 3 cups mixed greens with assorted raw veggies, 4 tsp oil and vinegar dressing

2 large or 6 regular crackers

Snack 1 fresh fruit

Dinner 1 soy burger on whole-wheat bun with 1 oz low-fat cheese, lettuce, onion, tomato, 1 tsp mustard, 2 tsp low-fat mayonnaise

1 oz baked chips

Snack 1 frozen juice bar

Day 13

Breakfast	Fruit smoothie
	Blend 6 oz silken tofu, ⅔ cup berries, 1 cup apple juice, 1 tsp vanilla, 1 small banana.
Lunch	Sandwich with 2 tbsp peanut butter and 2 tsp jelly
	Raw veggies
Snack	1 fresh fruit
Dinner	6 oz grilled steak
	1 medium baked potato with 2 tsp butter, 2 tbsp sour cream, and/or 1 tbsp shredded low-fat cheese
	Mixed green salad with 1 tbsp dressing of choice
Snack	½ cup low-fat ice cream

Day 14

Breakfast	Open-faced turkey and cheese melt
	On each slice of bread: 1-oz slice turkey and 1 slice fat-free cheese. Broil until cheese is melted.
	4 oz fruit juice
Lunch	1 cup low-fat cottage cheese
	½ cup canned fruit
	2 slices toast
Snack	6 oz low-sodium vegetable juice
Dinner	1 Salmon Patty*
	½ cup cooked green peas
	1 serving Baked Sweet Potato Wedges (see Day 7)
Snack	1 cup fresh or canned pineapple chunks

---

*Salmon Patties (serves 4)

1 15-oz can salmon, drained	12 unsalted saltines crushed
2 eggs	2 tbsp finely chopped onions or onion flakes
1 tbsp lemon juice	1 tbsp dried parsley

Mix all ingredients and form into 4 patties. Heat 2 tbsp canola oil in skillet over medium heat. Brown patties about 5 minutes per side. Serve topped with 1 tbsp catsup or tartar sauce.

Day 15

Breakfast

2 eggs

2 slices toast

1 fresh fruit

Lunch

Turkey and spinach wrap

1 whole-wheat low-carb tortilla, 3 oz turkey breast meat,
½ cup baby spinach leaves, 1 tbsp light dressing

Raw veggies

1 fresh fruit

Snack

1 oz low-fat cheese

2 large high-fiber crackers

Dinner

1 serving Beef and Broccoli Sauté (see Day 2)

½ cup brown rice, steamed or cooked in water or broth

Salad with mixed greens and assorted raw vegetables

2 tbsp oil and vinegar dressing

Snack

½ cup sherbet

Day 16

Breakfast

1 cup cereal with skim milk and 2 tbsp ground flaxseed

1 slice toast

1 fresh fruit

Lunch

Fish salad

3 oz water-packed tuna or sardines, 1 tsp lemon juice, 1 tbsp pickle relish, 1 tbsp creamy mustard

4 large or 12 small crackers

Raw veggies

1 fresh fruit

Snack

¼ cup unsalted roasted almonds

2 tbsp raisins or chopped dates

Dinner

1 grilled chicken breast marinated in teriyaki sauce

1 small baked potato plain or with butter substitute and 1 tbsp brown sugar

½ cup spinach sautéed in olive oil and chopped garlic

1 whole-wheat roll

1 fresh fruit

Snack

1 fudge Popsicle

Day 17

Breakfast   1 cup cereal with skim milk and 2 tbsp ground flaxseed

½ cup berries

1 slice toast

Lunch   Sub sandwich

6" whole-grain roll, 3 oz turkey, fresh veggie toppings, oil and vinegar dressing, pepper

1½ oz baked wheat chips

Snack   1 fresh fruit

1 oz mozzarella cheese stick

Dinner   4 oz roasted pork tenderloin brushed with olive oil, chopped garlic, thyme, and pepper

3 small new potatoes halved and roasted with meat

1 cup steamed broccoli sprinkled with lemon juice

½ cup cooked carrots seasoned with basil and olive oil

Snack   1 fresh fruit

Day 18

Breakfast	1 egg
	4 4-inch whole-wheat pancakes with 3 tbsp syrup
	1 fresh fruit
Lunch	1 cup low-fat, low-sodium soup
	Turkey sandwich
	2 slices bread, 4 oz turkey, 1 slice nonfat cheese, lettuce, 1–2 tomato slices, 1 tsp mustard
Snack	Raw veggies
Dinner	4 oz grilled or baked fish fillet, seasoned to taste
	½ cup brown rice
	5 asparagus spears steamed and sprinkled with lemon juice
	1 broiled tomato with low-fat feta cheese on top
	1 dinner roll
Snack	6 oz low-fat vanilla yogurt
	1 fresh fruit

Day 19

Breakfast	2 slices toast with 2 tbsp peanut butter and 2 tsp honey or jelly
	1 fresh fruit
Lunch	1 cup low-fat, low-sodium soup
	10 unsalted saltine crackers
Snack	1 fresh fruit
Dinner	1 Taco Salad in Baked Tortilla Bowl (see Day 10)
Snack	1 fresh fruit

Day 20

Breakfast	1 cup cooked oatmeal with skim milk and 2 tsp honey
	Add 2 tbsp chopped walnuts, 2 tbsp ground flaxseed
	1 fresh fruit
Lunch	Grilled chicken salad
	4 oz grilled chicken breast strips, 3 cups mixed greens with assorted raw veggies, 4 tsp oil and vinegar dressing
	2 large or 6 regular crackers
Snack	1 fresh fruit
Dinner	1 soy burger on whole-wheat bun with 1 oz low-fat cheese, lettuce, onion, tomato, 1 tsp mustard, 2 tsp low-fat mayonnaise
	1 oz baked chips
Snack	1 frozen juice bar

Day 21

Breakfast   Omelet with 2 eggs, mushrooms, onions, tomatoes, 1 oz shredded low-fat cheese

4 oz fruit juice

Lunch   Toasted chicken salad sandwich

Mix and spread between two slices of toast 3 oz canned chicken, 2 tbsp chopped celery, 1 tbsp chopped onion, 2 tbsp low-fat mayonnaise or salad dressing. Add two tomato slices and lettuce.

Snack   2 tbsp raisins

Dinner   Marinated and Grilled Flank Steak (see Day 11)

1 corn on the cob, boiled and unsalted

Mixed green salad with assorted raw veggies with oil and vinegar dressing

1 fresh fruit

Snack   ½ cup fat-free pudding

21

Spiritual Energy In: 90-Day Bible Reading Plan

Bible passages you can "feed on" during your 90-Day Challenge.

The following Bible passages, arranged into a 90-day reading plan, have been selected to nourish and energize your spiritual heart during your 90-Day Challenge. Each day, enter the reference for the passage you read on your Total Heart Health Journal page. As you read, be sensitive to what God is saying to you and what He is telling you do. Write your response in the spaces provided on the journal sheet.

Genesis 6
Genesis 7
Genesis 8
Genesis 9
Luke 1
Matthew 3
Matthew 11
Matthew 14:1–12
Genesis 12
Genesis 13
Genesis 14
Genesis 15
Genesis 22
Matthew 4
Matthew 10:1–15
Matthew 10:16–23
Matthew 10:24–42
Genesis 25:19–34
Genesis 27
Genesis 28

Genesis 32
Matthew 16:13–28
Luke 5:4–11
Matthew 14:22–36
Luke 22:31–38;
   Matthew 26:34–35,
   69–75
Genesis 37
Genesis 39
Genesis 40
Genesis 41:1–37
Genesis 41:38–57
Genesis 42
Genesis 43
Genesis 44
Genesis 45
Acts 9
Galatians 1:11–24
2 Corinthians 11:24–33;
   2 Corinthians 12

Exodus 1
Exodus 2
Exodus 3
Exodus 6:1–13; 7:1–8
Exodus 12
Exodus 20
Deuteronomy 34
2 Timothy 4
1 Timothy 1
1 Timothy 2
1 Timothy 3
1 Timothy 4
1 Timothy 5
1 Timothy 6
Numbers 14
Numbers 27:15–23
Deuteronomy 31
Joshua 1
Joshua 3
Joshua 5:13; 6

2 Timothy 1
2 Timothy 2
2 Timothy 3
2 Timothy 4
1 Samuel 16
1 Samuel 17
2 Samuel 1; 2:1–7
2 Samuel 7
2 Samuel 11
2 Samuel 12
Psalm 51
Philemon

Daniel 1
Daniel 2:1–30
Daniel 2:31–49
Daniel 3
Daniel 6
Romans 6
Romans 7
Romans 8
Nehemiah 1
Nehemiah 2
Nehemiah 3
Nehemiah 4

Nehemiah 5
Nehemiah 6
1 Corinthians 11:1–3;
    Ephesians 5
Psalm 78
Matthew 20
Psalm 1
John 15
John 17
Revelation 4–5

Notes

Chapter 1: You Gotta Have Heart—Total Heart

1. Kerby Anderson, "Health and Church Attendance," Probe Ministries, www.probe.org/docs/c-health2.html (accessed August 28, 2004).

Chapter 3: The Unique Nature of a Man's Spiritual Heart

1. Mary K. Pratt, "She's the boss: Women dominate relocation industry," *Boston Business Journal*, August 2, 2002.

2. John Eldredge, *Wild at Heart* (Nashville: Thomas Nelson, 2001), 10.

Chapter 4: Caught in the Cross Hairs

1. Rick Warren, *The Purpose Driven Life* (Grand Rapids: Zondervan, 2002), 23.

Chapter 5: The Hidden Killer

1. Centers for Disease Control/National Center for Health Statistics, as cited on http://www.americanheart.org (accessed January 15, 2005).

2. Ibid.

3. American Heart Association, *1999 Heart and Stroke Statistical Update* (1993):4.

4. American Heart Association, *1999 Heart and Stroke Statistical Update* (1998):4.

5. American Heart Association, *2003 Heart and Stroke Statistical Update* (2002):4.

6. Ibid.

7. Ibid., 12.

8. *Social Science & Medicine* 52 (2001):1565; *Journal of the American Medical Association* 281 (1999):901; *American Journal of Respiratory and Critical Care Medicine* (1998):175.

9. J. Herlitz et. al., "Mortality Risk Indications of Death, Mode of Death and Symptoms of Angina Pectoris During 5 Years After Coronary Bypass Grafting in Men and Women," *Journal of Internal Medicine* 247 (2000):500–506.

10. V. Vaccarino et al., "Sex Differences in Hospital Mortality After Coronary Artery Bypass Surgery: Evidence for a Higher Mortality in Younger Women," *Circulation* 105 (2002):1176–81. G. Christakis et al., "Is Body Size the Cause of Poor Outcomes of Coronary Artery Bypass Operations in Women?" *Journal of Thoracic and Cardiovascular Surgery* 110 (1995):1344–58. L. Fisher et al., "Association of Sex, Physical Size and Operative Mortality After Coronary Artery Bypass in Coronary

Artery Surgery (CASS)," *Journal of Thoracic and Cardiovascular Surgery* 84 (1982):334–41. F. Edwards et al., "Impact of Gender on Coronary Bypass Operative Mortality," *Annals of Thoracic Surgery* 66 (1998):125–312.

Chapter 7: As Your Stomach Goes, So Goes Your Heart

1. "AOA Fast Facts: What Is Obesity?" American Obesity Association, www.obesity.org (accessed September 16, 2004).

2. "AOA Facts Sheet: Obesity in the U.S.," American Obesity Association, www.obesity.org (accessed September 16, 2004).

3. Centers for Disease Control, *National Center for Health Statistics, National Health and Nutrition Examination Survey*, "Health, United States" (Table 70) 2002.

4. Ibid.

5. Ibid.

6. "What Is Obesity?" American Obesity Association, www.obesity.org.

7. Walter C. Willett, MD, *Eat, Drink, and Be Healthy: The Harvard Medical School Guide to Healthy Eating* (New York: Free Press, 2001).

Chapter 8: Are the Calories You Eat Working for You or Against You?

1. www.nwcr.com (accessed August 28, 2004).

2. M. L. Klem, R. R. Wing, M. T. McGuire, H. M. Seagle, and J. O. Hill, "A Descriptive Study of Individuals Successful at Long-Term Maintenance of Substantial Weight Loss," *American Journal of Clinical Nutrition* 66 (1977):239–46.

Chapter 10: Five Myths Leading to Spiritual Anemia

1. Rick Warren, *The Purpose Driven Life* (Grand Rapids: Zondervan, 2002), 282.

2. Samuel Shoemaker, *Extraordinary Living for Ordinary Men* (Grand Rapids: Zondervan, 1965), 158–60.

Chapter 12: Fueling Up for a Stronger Heart

1. A. Ascherio, M. B. Katan, P. L. Zock, M. J. Stamphfer, W. C. Willett, "Trans Fatty Acids and Coronary Heart Disease," *New England Journal of Medicine* 340 (1999):1994–98.

2. C. M. Albert, H. Campos, M. J. Stampfer, et al., "Blood Levels of Long-Chain n-3 Fatty Acids and the Risk of Sudden Death," *New England Journal of Medicine* 346 (2002):1113–18.

3. "Early Protection Against Sudden Death by n-3 Polyunsaturated Fatty Acids After Miocardial Infarction: Time-Course Analysis of the Results of the GISSI Prevensione," *Circulation* 105 (2002):1897–1903.

4. F. B. Hu, L. Bronner, W. C. Willett, et al., "Fish and Omega 3 Fatty Acid Intake and Risk of Coronary Heart Disease in Women," *Journal of the American Medical Association* 287 (2002):1815–21.

Chapter 13: Fuel Additives That Can Increase Performance

1. Eugene Braunwald, Anthony S. Fauci, Dennis L. Kasper, Stephen L. Hauser, Dan L. Longo, J. Larry Jameson, eds. *Harrison's Principles of Internal Medicine,* 14th ed. (New York: McGraw-Hill, 1998), 446.

Chapter 14: Running in the Fast Lane

1. "Brack Steals 83rd Indy After Gordon Runs Out of Fuel," www.cnnsi.com, posted August 16, 1999.

2. http://www.harvestprayer.com/pray101/pmen.html (accessed September 5, 2004).

Chapter 16: Power with a Purpose

1. Rick Warren, *The Purpose Driven Life* (Grand Rapids: Zondervan, 2002), 283–84.

2. Antonio Porchia, *Voices* (Port Townsend, Wash.: Copper Canyon Press, 2003), 91.

Chapter 17: The Buck for Your Healthy Diet Stops Here

1. "Comparison of the Atkins, Ornish, Weight Watchers, and Zone Diets for Weight Loss and Heart Disease Risk Reduction—a Randomized Trial," *Journal of the American Medical Association* 293 (2005):43–53.

Chapter 18: The Many Voices Influencing Your Masculinity

1. Many versions of this humorous story are in circulation. This version was retrieved from http://my.homewithgod.com/mkcathy/humor/gender.html on February 9, 2005.

2. "Obsessed with Sex: How Kinsey's fraudulent science unleashed a catastrophic 'revolution,'" November 2004, *WorldNetDaily.*

3. Bruce Thompson, "The Modern World's Greatest Delusion," *National Review,* December 19, 2004.

4. Dean Hamer, *The God Gene* (New York: Doubleday, 2004), 17.

5. While documentation has not been found of Chesterton's response, the American Chesterton Society assumes that it actually happened. See http://www.chesterton.org/qmeister2/wrongtoday.htm.

Chapter 19: Are You Ready for the 90-Day Challenge?

1. The Cooper Institute, "How People Change: Psychological Theories & The Transtheoretical Model for Behavioral Change," 2003.

2. For a detailed plan of action and journal, get *The Total Heart Health for Men Workbook* (Nashville: Thomas Nelson, 2005).

3. For additional Bible reading and meditation resources, purchase *365 Days of Total Heart Health* (Nashville: Thomas Nelson, 2005). This is a devotional guide for each day of the year, complete with practical tips for spiritual and physical heart health.

Chapter 20: Physical Energy In

1. P. M. Kris-Etherton, W. S. Harris, L. J. Appel, "Omega-3 Fatty Acids and Cardiovascular Disease. New Recommendations from the American Heart Association," *Arteriosclerosis, Thrombosis, and Vascular Biology* 23 (2003):151–52.

A New You in 90 Days

Ed and JoBeth Young of the
Second Baptist Church of Houston,
along with two of the nation's
leading cardiologists, Michael
Duncan and Richard Leachman,
have developed the Total Heart
Health system, a program that insures
you keep a balanced focus on your
physical and spiritual health with:

SATISFACTION GUARANTEED!
If after completing the 90-Day
Total Heart Health Challenge
you aren't satisfied, we'll refund the
the purchase price of the trade
book.*
*offer not valid for Workbooks
or Devotional

- ◆ Fitness Tips
- ◆ Smart Recipes
- ◆ Daily Devotions
- ◆ Tools to become your
  own health & fitness coach
- ◆ A 90-Day Total Heart Health Challenge
- ◆ All around strategies for better living

www.thomasnelson.com

NELSON IMPACT

W PUBLISHING GROUP

COUNTRYMAN

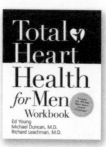

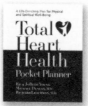